Not a Victim

Enable your child to

break through bullying

and develop a black belt in resilience for life

Sebastian Bates   Menno Siebinga

Re think

First published in Great Britain in 2021
by Rethink Press (www.rethinkpress.com)

Contents

Introduction

The tragedy of bullying is that so many children go through it alone for far too long, without the support and mentoring they need. We have seen the heartache, hopelessness and helplessness that parents experience as they watch their children go through bullying, not knowing when it will stop or how to help, many of them believing that they have tried everything, and nothing will work. Sadly, children are more likely to experience bullying than not and it's our responsibility as parents to prepare and empower them. By doing so, you radically improve their confidence, give them a strong positive inner voice and build their emotional intelligence.

This book will give you the motivation and tools to tackle bullying head on in the form of a proven,

practical guide. The Not A Victim process is the culmi-
nation of a decade of practical knowledge, experience
and real-life results in mentoring thousands of young
people through bullying. It is the ultimate guide for
any parent when it comes to bullying. Our own experiences of bullying have led to a deep shared passion for mentoring young people. It led Sebastian to
founding the Warrior Academy, where we work with
parents to enable their child overcome bullying, and
to Menno founding 'Body & Brein', where we work
with adults to enable them to continue to achieve
their goals as they mature. The Not A Victim process
was originally a four-step method called the Warrior
Method; over the years, it evolved into six steps and
we decided to turn it into this book.

This book is made up of three parts. The first part
provides you with the background to bullying, why
it occurs, the different forms it can take – physical,
mental and emotional, both offline and online – the
signs that your child is being bullied, when it's likely
to happen, the problems it can cause and the effects it
can have on the brain.

The second part delves into the advice on how to deal
with bullying, our easy-to-implement process for
achieving a black belt in resilience, consisting of the
6Ps: six practical steps that you can take right away
to mentor your child through overcoming bullying.
We have used these steps successfully with hundreds
of families. The majority of children overcome their

bullying before they reach step three, but it's crucial to follow all six steps to ensure that the bullying does not recur, that your child does not become a bully themselves and that their character is fully developed. Finally, the third part of the book explains what breaking through bullying will mean to you and your child, how it can be a turning point in your child's life, developing their character and setting them up well for dealing with the challenges of life.

Throughout the book, you will read in the Bullying Breakthroughs about incredibly successful individuals who have experienced bullying, and how they broke through it to achieve success in life – how their pain became their strength. Their inspiring stories will give you a deeper understanding of the effects of bullying and what other people have done to overcome it.

If you've just found out that your child is being or has been bullied and realise that something needs to happen *now*, we suggest you go straight to Part Two and start applying the 6Ps, until you begin to see a change. When you are in a calmer space and state, read the book from beginning to end. It will prepare you and your family to break the cycle of bullying and overcome other life obstacles along the way. Our vision is of a world in which it is normal for parents to equip their child with the tools to break through bullying and other obstacles, just as they teach them to brush their teeth, so that their child can thrive in life, no matter what. Through mentoring, you can support your child to step away from becoming the victim of a cycle that can repeat into adulthood. This book is intended to support you and your child, providing an opportunity for introspection and enlightenment as well as practical guidance that will give your child a black belt in resilience for life.

PART ONE
THE WORLD OF BULLYING

Our work with young people over the last decade suggests that a child is more likely to be bullied than not. Instances of bullying have increased with the rise of cyberbullying, where an individual can hide behind an alias without risk of detection. This first part of the book will help you to understand the importance of community. If a child is surrounded by a negative community, they are more likely to be bullied, while a positive community will provide emotional support. Bullying is not a one-off event; it is a transition that carries with it important life lessons on how to deal with confrontation, stand up for ourselves, show courage and confidence, and follow our own judgement.

BULLYING BREAKTHROUGH 1: SEBASTIAN

The first major bullying I experienced occurred between the ages of seven and eleven, during the first big transition in my life, changing schools. Not from primary to secondary school but due to a house move. My new school was in a rural town with few children, very different from what I was used to. It was run by an elderly married couple with traditional teaching methods and an 'old school' approach. Each class had roughly a dozen students, with tight-knit friendship groups and clear pecking orders. The other students in my class were ahead of me academically, and the teachers' efforts to improve my work only widened the divide. I was also, of course, the 'new kid' and fairly small for my age. The stage was perfectly set for bullying.

It started verbally, with name calling, followed by segregation and isolation during break. I was picked last for every game, not invited to birthday parties and so on. Where previously after school I'd be out playing with other children in the neighbourhood, now I'd come home and play alone. Although quite a confident boy by nature, I soon became more introverted, shy and unsure of myself.

I remember vividly how I was cleverly targeted, out of sight of teachers. I remember the fear of rejection and the uncertainty about how the day would go. My behaviour worsened as I tried to impress the other boys by acting up in front of teachers. I began to disregard and resent authority as I noticed others getting away with terrible behaviour (directed at me). I spent a lot of my time standing outside the headmistress's office with my nose against the wall and my hands behind my back. My progress in school worsened, for which I was punished at home.

To build my confidence, my parents enrolled me in a martial arts club. We can only understand the importance of certain points in our lives when we look back. This was one of those moments. When I first stepped into the dojo to watch a taekwondo class, I remember the sense of relief, excitement and, more than anything, hope. I watched in awe as black belts performed drills with incredible flexibility, speed and strength. I wanted to be them. I had to be them.

At the martial arts club, I was part of a community where courtesy and respect were valued and developing a positive mindset was expected. I was able to speak freely about what I was going through and build the strength of character I needed to overcome bullying.

And yet, the bullying intensified. It turned physical. At one point, I was held and repeatedly kicked between the legs by the ringleader. Winning a trophy at my first national championships filled both me and my parents with pride. But when my teacher asked me to show it to the class and I left it under my desk, the bullies destroyed it. Heartbroken, I threw the pieces in the bin.

My parents were now finally aware of the bullying. Even as a nine-year-old, I'd felt ashamed, almost guilty, talking to them about it. Now, having worked with so many young children in this situation, I understand how normal that feeling is – perhaps even more so for boys, given the stereotypical expectation to 'be strong'. It was my parents' worst nightmare. They tried everything – speaking to the school, the teachers, the other parents, but they had little proof. I was given a 'bully book' to write in details of incidents – eventually, this was found by the bullies and you can only imagine how much worse that made things. Having reached his tipping point, my father walked into the school to address the students and my teacher, but to no avail.

I think deep down they knew that removing me from the situation would stop the bullying, but it wouldn't teach me to overcome it on my own. Incredibly, they poured their energy into giving me the tools, the confidence and the techniques I needed. Four years after my ordeal began, I had a strong sense of self-worth and was equipped with a newly developed moral compass. I simply couldn't stand the injustice and developed the courage to stand up to my aggressors.

I often find with our young students that there is one defining moment when they take a stand, which fills them with empowerment and resilience. For me, this defining moment was when one of the boys tripped me up during a game of football and my head hit a concrete floor. I got up and retaliated, using techniques I had learned from martial arts. In that moment I was transformed. I saw the weakness in the bully's eyes, and it was as if the roles were reversed. I realised in that moment that I didn't have to be a victim.

Looking back, I can see that the most powerful contributors to this transition were the mentoring I received from my parents and the consistent support I had from my martial arts community.

When I transitioned from primary to secondary school, I was bullied again. But this time I had the tools to overcome it on my own. I went on to become a third-degree black belt, professional Muay Thai fighter and win multiple national champions, studying six different styles of martial arts. My success gave me the confidence to take on all kinds of challenges across the world.

My experience is a classic example of how significant transitions can lead to years of emotional distress, flying under the parents' radar. But it's also an example of post-traumatic growth. Of how going through such a terrible ordeal can help us evolve.

I had no idea at the time that this traumatic experience would propel me towards what I later achieved in life. Only when looking back can we join up the dots and see that our pain has become our strength.

BULLYING BREAKTHROUGH 2: MENNO

At primary school, I was the smallest boy in the class. Despite being my friends, the other boys teased me for being the smallest. I couldn't handle it and would get angry. I told them to stop, which only made it worse; the bullying continued almost every day. I don't remember being supported by my teacher, or if he saw what was happening. The bullying continued relentlessly until I started high school. I only had sports as a way of letting off steam.

In my first class at high school, I made friends with a boy on the same football team as me. He had red hair and was teased for it. But he was a bully himself, and it started again. This time, though, it was different. Before, I had always told my bullies to stop. I had never reacted physically, maybe because I was so small; I was scared, worrying about what might happen if I did. Again, I asked my bully to stop, but he didn't. Finally, I got so angry that I snapped and retaliated physically.

This was a scary moment. I didn't know what I was doing. It's frightening when you are pushed so far that it feels like you no longer have control over your actions and emotions, and you do something you might regret.

Looking back, I realise that I didn't know what these boys' intentions were. Was it just teasing or were they intending to bully me? The effect on me was the same; I couldn't tell the difference and was badly affected.

Even after my physical retaliation, the bullying didn't stop. I began to turn into an aggressive kid. The crazy thing is, I didn't know it was happening, because the change happened gradually.

My grades weren't hugely affected, because I loved learning and still do, but at thirteen, I began displaying disruptive behaviour, hanging out with the wrong crowd, staying out at night and drinking. I acted tough, or so I thought. When a bigger and older guy looked at me or approached me, I would ask him what he was looking at. They would never react, just walk away, which I saw as a victory. Looking back, this was wrong; they probably saw a small, insecure kid who wasn't worth picking on. Nevertheless, it gave me a false sense of security.

I kept acting like this until one day I got into a physical altercation outside a nightclub, initiated by me, only this time the other guy didn't walk away. He was much older and bigger than me. He grabbed me by the throat with one hand and pulled back the other hand to hit me in the face. I leaned back and tried to kick him. He walked away, but five minutes later returned with three of his friends, also much older and bigger than me and my friend and challenged us to a fight. Fortunately, a bouncer arrived and pulled us apart.

This was a turning point, because I realised I had to back up my big mouth. I couldn't fight, and if I kept behaving like this, I was going to get hurt. That summer, I saw in the local newspaper that a new martial arts centre was opening a few miles from my village. My father drove me there and my love affair with martial arts began. It would change me, but not yet.

The next change came as a result of a comment by my best female friend, who probably didn't have any idea how big an impact her words would have on me. One day, she looked at me and asked, 'Why do you always look so mad?' I was gobsmacked, because I'd had no idea I looked this way. I pondered her comment for days and realised she was right. But not only did I look mad, I felt mad, all the time.

After this realisation I slowly began to change. I didn't look mad anymore, I went to clubs to have fun, not to act tough or to pick fights. I didn't get into trouble anymore, but the bullying didn't stop. Not yet. Other boys continued to bully me, but it didn't affect me the same way, so the fun went out of it for them. They also knew that I was doing martial arts and was pretty fanatical about it, which intimidated them.

I also stopped hanging out with the wrong crowd and making poor choices, which were impacting my health. Martial arts triggered an interest in all kinds of physical and mental activities. I started reading books and watching movies, developing a particular fascination with Bruce Lee. I wanted to study either the mind or the body, which eventually led to my choosing to study physiotherapy.

My continued thirst for learning different kinds of martial arts led me to study and practise eight martial arts and become a teacher of four of them. When I graduated as a physiotherapist, I wanted to travel the world and study martial arts in different countries. This experience changed me even further. From a largely introverted boy, I became a much more extroverted man. I decided I wanted to compete in martial arts and eventually became a world champion – the first the island I lived on had ever produced.

When I was working as a physio, I experienced two moments of reflection and realisation. The first was while I was treating a woman's back. For some reason, the conversation turned to her husband and, when she mentioned his name, my jaw dropped. She had married the guy who'd picked that fight with me at the club. I said to her, 'When you go home, please thank your husband for picking a fight with me, because that set me onto the path of martial arts, and then to physiotherapy, and even to becoming a world champion.'

The second came a few years later, when I took on an older female patient. As soon as I introduced myself, she started crying. She told me how her son had been badly bullied by me and my brother in elementary school, that he came home crying and aggressive day after day. Now he was a strong person and a happily married man. She said he could take me on. I kept my mouth shut and listened. I didn't have any recollection of bullying her son and had no idea of the extent to which I had affected him and his mother.

The work I do with Sebastian is part of my mission to
close this circle in an attempt to stop children who are
bullied becoming bullies themselves.

1
The World Has Changed: Are You Ready?

While writing this book, we were working at an incredibly deep level with hundreds of parents whose children were facing bullying, through our Not A Victim workshops. Naively, when we began these workshops, we believed that parents would be ready and open to helping. That any initial insights parents could gain to help mentor their child through a difficult stage would be welcomed. We wanted to create a level of support that my parents had never had, that would have eased the pain, the helplessness and hopelessness that we saw in their eyes, just as we had seen in the hundreds of parents we had worked with previously.

Children don't go through bullying alone. It's a shared journey – the importance of which will become vividly clear.

Instead, we discovered that a huge number of parents were not ready to be helped. So, before we share with you our Not A Victim process, a system that has enabled hundreds to overcome bullying, we need to first ensure that you are ready to work with us, with your child and with yourself. At the workshops, we always know quickly who is ready and who is resistant based on their body language. A defensive posture with arms folded and avoiding eye contact indicates a reluctance to participate. It means that these parents are experiencing bullying; they are reliving bullying. Their defences are up, because as they have watched their children go through bullying, they have shared every moment of fear, pain, doubt, anxiety, depression, anger and frustration. If we are able to spot ourselves falling into this state, we have a better chance of engaging the neocortex of our brains, where our visionary mindset is located. Then, we are able to respond in the most positive way.[1] For parents of a child being bullied, that translates into mentoring your child from a far more positive position, with a more proactive and less reactive approach, which will accelerate the speed at which they make it through this difficult transition.

---

1   Brain Science, 'What is the limbic brain and how can you tap into its power?', Growth Engingeering (13 February 2020), www.growthengineering.co.uk/the-limbic-brain, accessed 27 May 2021

Managing emotional triggers

We all have emotional triggers. They are highly reactive places inside you that are instantly activated by a subject, situation, or someone else's behaviours or comments. A trigger subject can come up in conversation and we literally shut down. Someone can say something that makes us recall a memory or feeling and we react defensively or angrily. It's not a conscious decision; an emotional trigger has been pulled. If you, as a parent, have unaddressed insecurities or emotional triggers around the highly emotive subject of bullying, then you are likely to act differently, perhaps more defensively and definitely more reactively, to this subject. By recognising our emotional triggers, we can build a deeper understanding of why bullying occurs and how insecurities develop. We observe our behaviour (both verbal and non-verbal, ie body language) and, by spotting our triggers, can course-correct, choosing the behaviour that will give us the best chance of overcoming bullying quickly, with our child. It's important that we manage our emotional triggers, not just to help our child overcome bullying, but also for our personal development and self-awareness. Once we know our emotional triggers, we can start to understand why we make certain decisions or act in a certain way. As parents, we must accept our responsibility to mentor our child from a position of power, not of victimhood. If you are stuck in a victim mindset, your judgement, actions and mentoring will not come from a positive place. Consider how different your life would be if you were in complete control of your reactions, choosing emotional freedom and inspiring your child to do the same. We must let go of old baggage so that we do not pass it onto our child. Sometimes, this baggage can be hard to spot, so it's our duty, our responsibility, to dig deep into our past and ask some difficult questions. Whether you were previously bullied or not, the subject of bullying may still trigger a deeply reactive emotion. Try to discover the emotional triggers that have ultimately impacted the way you have lived your life.

Having a mindful conversation

One of the most important steps in combating bullying is opening the lines of communication. How can we help a child without knowing what they are going through?

A child can feel ashamed, embarrassed or guilty when they are being victimised and bullied. We have found that there is often an element of toxic masculinity, among young boys in particular. They do not want to admit to being bullied for fear of appearing weak. They believe their role is to be strong and 'masculine' and any deviation from this threatens their persona and role within the family. These feelings are amplified in many of the cultures we've worked within. Having so much technology and information readily at our disposal, plus all the attention-stealing devices we now take for granted, can be overwhelming. Have you ever been trying to do something, your child has come to you and you say, 'Not now'? All of us parents fall into this trap on occasion, even while knowing our child is more important than whatever activity we're in the middle of. We need to make sure that our child knows they can come to us with whatever is on their mind, big or small, at any time. A good idea is to introduce a word or sentence that you and your child decide on, which will let you know that your child needs your full attention. It's important that you have a system in place before it is needed, because when a child is troubled by something, they can have doubts about whether to address it, or might feel too ashamed to bring it up. If the process begins too late, when they do share, it is often more challenging and can become a guessing game. Communication is always more challenging when there are emotions involved.

Fortunately, this is an action you can take straightaway.

The magic button

Pick a moment to have a conversation with your child. Tell them that when something is challenging, they can try to figure it out for themselves, but if they need you, you will be there, no matter the time or situation. Together, come up with a word or sentence that will be your 'magic button' for prompting a conversation about anything that is bothering them. After you have established this magic button, remind your child of it regularly, otherwise doubt can kick in and they won't use it. Once you've had the initial conversation, it's important to establish a routine where you check in with your child on a regular basis.

If your child does 'press the magic button', make them a priority. Be fully present, turn off all technology and focus completely on the conversation to be had. Listen to what your child is saying without judgement, without reaction, criticism or defensiveness. Try to identify the problem, then discuss it and look for ways to solve it, now and forever. Be realistic about the fact that it might take time. If you are lucky enough to have your parents – or whoever mentored or raised you – still around, or you have teachers or friends you can speak to, have a mindful conversation with them too. Ask your parents what school was like for them. Were they ever picked on or bullied?

Our generation, and certainly our parents' generation, had a 'kids will be kids' mindset and pushed bullying to the side without looking into what was causing it or how to prevent it. It was considered part of growing up and something we couldn't stop, so shouldn't bother tackling. This does make asking your parents about their bullying experiences (or even thinking about your own) difficult. These questions may be more effective if they are not specifically about bullying and instead approach the subject from different angles. Questions such as:

- Did you have lots of friends at school?

- Who was your best friend?

- Did you ever find changing schools difficult?

- Did you struggle to fit into new social groups?

- What did you look like/how did you dress when you were younger?

- Did anyone ever comment on how you looked?

- What was your nickname at school?

- Can you remember the first time you felt embarrassed? Can you talk about that? How did you feel?

When listening to the answers, remember to respond but not react. Immerse yourself in every word and every feeling. It's up to you to make the conversation as comfortable for them as possible.

After this mindful conversation with your parents, you are likely to have a far deeper understanding of their position and of how and why they raised you the way they did. You may even realise that you need to forgive them in order to grow yourself. Parenting can be much like bullying, a flow of negativity. The way we parent is determined by our experiences, and ultimately our emotional triggers. It is our duty as parents to recognise and address these.

Spotting an emotional reaction

Neuroscientist Antonio Damasio, author of *Looking for Spinoza: Joy, Sorrow and the Feeling Brain*,[2] states that whenever you notice a change in your breathing, in the blood flow in your stomach, or in muscle tension, this represents an emotional pattern that you can identify as a 'feeling'. It will manifest in your body language almost immediately. If you feel defensive, your arms will cross, and your mind will close – just like the parents we mentioned earlier in this chapter. Do not judge or fear these feelings or emotions. Instead, understand that they are normal and ask yourself, what triggered this response? Was it fear, sadness, anger, anxiety? In that precise moment, was there something that you felt was missing? Being emotionally triggered almost always comes back to a deep-rooted desire or need that isn't being fulfilled. What was it?

- Being in control

- Being liked

- Being right

- Peacefulness

- Predictability

- Acceptance

---

2   A Damasio, *Looking for Spinoza: Joy, Sorrow and the Feeling Brain* (Harvest, 2003)

- Attention

- Love

- Being needed

- Safety

- Fun

- Consistency

- Respect

- Being treated fairly

- Being valued

Being honest with yourself, are you able to spot your reaction and link it to an unmet desire or need? These needs are not bad; they are important and at some point in your life they were vital. What is less important and can be damaging is your attachment to these needs. An unmet need, a lack of something, can become the emotional trigger that prevents you, and ultimately your child, from experiencing growth, inspiration and fulfilment. It holds you, and them, back. Next, ask yourself:

- Am I *really* missing this need or want?

- Is the person who has triggered this reaction *really* taking this from me?

- Am I reacting too personally to the suggestion of something, the words or the subject?

- Is this person trying to help me or hinder me?

- Are they working with me, for the same cause, or against me?

Decide which feeling you *want* to experience and shift your emotional state by:

1. Choosing a physical response to the emotional trigger.

2. Focusing on your breathing as you feel this emotion arise, slowly breathing in through your nose for five seconds, holding your breath for five seconds and breathing out for ten seconds. If this is too difficult, change the number of seconds, keeping the same rhythm, so two-second inhale, two-second hold, four-second exhale. The most important thing is the after-effect we want to create.

3. Calming your body, clearing your thoughts and releasing tension.

4. Choosing a new emotion, such as 'relaxed', 'happy', 'excited', ensuring that, whatever you choose, it's positive and provides you with the foundation to move forward, proactively.

As you work through this book, we want you to shift your emotional state and focus on your visionary mindset. Engage your neocortex and learn to spot your emotional triggers, as and when they arise (and they will, as you read on).

Proactivity vs reactivity

In our work, we've found that most parents aren't proactive when it comes to bullying and obstacles their child faces. Some see a lack of self-defence mechanisms, so they put their child in a martial arts class, expecting it to fix this. But the threat is not always an immediate or physical one. In this technology age, we can be attacked from anywhere, by anyone, at any time. Before, when a child came home from school, they would be in a safe environment. Now, as soon as they open a device, they are open to attack. This is another reason we wrote this book, to equip parents like you with the 'martial arts of the twenty-first century', which will prepare your child for attack, whether physical, mental or digital.

As parents, we are protective of our child because we know what's out there and don't want them to have bad experiences. We want them to feel happy and confident. We all know that life is not filled only with happy moments. We will all suffer our share of pain, loss and grief. Those moments and how we handle them will shape us and determine how we manage similar events in the future. As parents we have a role to play in helping our child become self-reliant – not only when they feel good, but also when they don't.

Because pain is not comfortable, people can try to avoid social interaction or hide behind an external stimulus – gaming or binge-watching TV, for example – to avoid feeling it. These stimuli may numb the pain, but it will only rise again later. Sometimes we rush through our pain to get past it, but pain comes with essential learning. If we choose to learn from it, pain often becomes the reason we want to change.

We need to teach our child that it is normal to feel pain, to feel sad, angry or anxious. These states are not bad or good. It's about not staying in that state longer than necessary or using it for the basis of our actions, because this will make us function inefficiently. We must learn how to respond to those states appropriately and how to regulate them, to reduce the chance of their reoccurrence.

We have all heard about soldiers coming back from war with post-traumatic stress disorder (PTSD). They don't suffer this *during* the war, because they are trained and prepared for war; the problems arise when they come home. Though there is no external threat, they remain on high alert. They feel anxious, have a hard time falling asleep and cannot focus. They have difficulty regulating their internal state, and often don't realise that they have any control over this. Research has shown that bullying can be one of the strongest factors in developing PTSD symptoms.[3]

---

3   S Matthiesen and S Einarson, 'Psychiatric distress and symptoms of PTSD among victims of bullying at work', *British Journal of Guidance & Counselling*, 32/3, (2010), https://doi.org/10.1080/03069880410001 723558, accessed 7 May 2021

We must teach our child that it's okay to feel bad; the important thing is being able to respond appropriately to that feeling. Learning how to tolerate feeling bad and still being able to function. If we can do this, it will massively decrease the chance of our child being bullied or bullying others. This is also important from the perspective of self-protection. When a child is left out, it doesn't feel good. The child may think that there is something wrong with them. We have to teach them how to read and regulate such feelings and diagnose the real issue, so that a solution can be found and tolerance developed. All progress is accompanied by moments of not feeling good, moments of frustration, despair, wanting to give up. This is how we grow and evolve. Sports psychologist Michael Gervais puts it eloquently: 'Pain is the reason we change. Discomfort is the reason we grow.'[4]

We have found that even when the external bullying stops, the bullying that happens inside your child often continues. They may have negative self-talk and low self-confidence and will shy away from challenges. It's hugely important to address all the negative effects of bullying. If your child is not prepared to deal with a bully, the bully will exploit their position of power, which will put your child at more of a disadvantage. That's why preparation is so important. Both you and your child must know what to do

---

4   M Gervais, 'The real reason we change', Victory Performance and Physical Therapy Blog (20 November 2020), www.victoryperformancept.com/blog/2020/11/20/the-real-reason-we-change, accessed 7 May 2021

if bullying occurs. Our aim is to prepare you and your child, so that you are in the best position to respond.

Dan Millman, a world champion athlete, has said, 'If, when playing an opponent, you are also opposing yourself, you will be outnumbered.'[5] Preparation ensures that your child doesn't outnumber themselves in a bullying situation. They know how to respond and know how to bounce back. Through preparation, your child will also learn to read threats and dangerous situations and to recognise their weak points. Like learning to cross the road, they will come to know what to look for and where to look. The best way to prevent bullying is to avoid getting into a situation where you might be bullied, and the best starting point is one of knowledge, not of fear. This puts your child ahead of the bully.

How ready are you?

To find out how prepared you and your child already are, we suggest completing our Bully Readiness Assessment at: www.notavictim.co.uk. It's a simple thirty 'yes/no' answer quiz that will provide you with a personalised professional breakdown of the different categories regarding becoming resilient to bullying. This will give you valuable insights into the areas you and your child need to develop and the areas to maintain in order to achieve a black belt in resilience

---

5   D Millman, *Way of the Peaceful Warrior: A Book That Changes Lives* (HJ Kramer, 1980)

and readiness. Don't worry if you get low scores. The purpose of this book is to enable you to improve your readiness; once you've read it, you can retake the quiz to see how much you have improved.

2
How Bullying Works

When we talk about bullying, it's common to think about other people bullying us and about physical pain. There's often less talk of the mental pain that bullying can cause. With physical pain, the healing process is not conscious; over time, it just happens. Healing mental pain is different, we need a conscious strategy for it, otherwise, we can create stories in our mind that will make us less likely to recover and become mentally strong. When your body feels sore, it's harder to move; it's the same with mental soreness, it makes it harder to think, decide and act. We want you to help your child to become resilient against both kinds of pain. Learning how to deal with the mental pain of bullying in particular will set your child up well for the twenty-first century.

Bullying and the brain

Bullying causes changes in brain function and brain structures, comparable to the harm done by chronic and acute stress. In fact, bullying can contribute to chronic stress, while witnessing or undergoing trauma is a form of acute stress. Scientists have found that bullying, child abuse, trauma and stress all cause comparable changes in particular parts of the brain.[6]

One of the most famous theories for understanding the brain is the triune brain theory, which was developed by Paul MacLean, became influential in the 1960s[7] and has been revised over the years since. This theory distinguishes three sections of the brain: the reptilian brain, the limbic system and the prefrontal cortex. The reptilian brain, the oldest of the three from an evolutionary perspective, includes the main structures found in a reptile's brain: the brainstem and the cerebellum. This brain is reliable but rigid; it's our 'fight or flight' mechanism. The limbic system, which emerged in mammals first, is more advanced. This section of the brain includes the hippocampus, the hypothalamus and the amygdala. It records memories of experiences and is responsible for our emotions, having a strong influence over our decisions and behaviour. Finally, the prefrontal cortex

---

6   G Nolfe et al, 'Bullying at workplace and brain-imaging correlates', *Journal of Clinical Medicine*, 7/8 (4 August 2018), 200, https://doi.org/10.3390/jcm7080200, accessed 7 May 2021

7   P MacLean, *The Triune Brain in Evolution: Role in paleocerebral functions* (Springer, 1990)

(PFC), which first evolved in primates and reached its highest evolutionary state in the human brain, incorporates two large cerebral hemispheres, which are the source of our abstract thinking, vision, creativity, imagination and language. The PFC is flexible with an infinite learning ability.

Of course, these three sections of the brain influence each other. It is essential to understand that the brain is developing from before birth until around age twenty-five. This development involves an increase in connections between nerve cells. During puberty, a pruning process occurs to retain the most useful connections and to optimise communication in the brain. Inactive connections disappear, and many well-used connections are strengthened. This optimisation process does not happen in all brain sections at once. The emotional brain (limbic system) is first up, as extra stimuli are generated by our hormones during adolescence. At this stage in our development, the rest of the brain is not strong enough to understand and control this hypersensitivity of the emotional brain, so the adolescent brain is out of balance, influencing adolescent behaviour.

Bullying, like stress, alters the chemical messengers in the brain: hormones and neurotransmitters (adrenalin, cortisol, vasopressin and serotonin are a few of them), which can be excitatory or inhibitory. When we are scared or experience a stressful event, high hormonal activity occurs immediately in the limbic system. The reptilian brain is activated, and we shut down the PFC, the part of our brain that is able to process visionary, creative ideas. We feel pessimistic, less likely to explore new concepts, and our defences go up, putting our body into the well-known 'fight or flight' mode. Physically, our body language changes, our heart rate increases, we take in more oxygen, our pupils dilate, our muscles tense. Our body is ready to take action. It's possible for people who are going through emotional trauma to live like this for days, weeks or months at a time and for the impact to be both short- and long-term). If we are able to spot ourselves falling into this state, we have a better chance of engaging the PFC and being able to respond in a positive way. As a parent experiencing the stress of your child being bullied, that translates into mentoring your child from a far more positive position, with a more proactive (less reactive) approach. This will accelerate the speed at which your child will make it through the bullying experience.

After the threat has gone, it takes twenty to sixty minutes for the body to return to its pre-arousal state. Neurotransmitters again govern this phase. This is a natural and healthy system in balance, which means that stress, in moderation, is not necessarily harmful. Things get complicated when a person experiences chronic stress. Bullying is mostly a systematic, chronic form of aggression. The careful balance between excitatory and inhibitory actions in the brain is lost when cortisol, the arousal hormone, stays at high levels.

High cortisol levels can damage certain brain structures and increase the size of others, which may result
in serious health problems, both psychological disorders (anxiety, depression, poor self-esteem) and physical disorders (high blood pressure, increased risk of
heart disease, diabetes). Over time, this can lead to
impulsive, even violent behaviour, increased anxiety,
depression, alcohol and drug abuse, learning disorders and stress-related diseases.

What is remarkable is the variety of responses to stress
in different individuals. A small amount of stress
related to a one-off event or situation can cause long-
lasting effects that can continue into adulthood (as
you'll remember from Menno's story), while substan-
tial or long-lasting situations can cause only mild and
transitory damage and symptoms. The consequences
of trauma are not always related to its severity, which
is why there is a wide variety in the extent of harm a
person will suffer from bullying.

These observations are essential when we look for
ways to heal the damage caused by bullying and
stress. How can we develop resilience? Or should
we focus on resistance? What neurobiological substances play a role here? Many researchers all over the
world are investigating this subject. As soon as there
is a better understanding of these issues, we will be
closer to a solution for the damage to the brain caused
by bullying and trauma. In contrast to earlier opinions, we know now that nerve cells can regenerate

(the survival and incorporation of new neurons is known as neuroplasticity).[8] We do not yet know, however, how to stimulate this process. Until we do, we embrace a variety of valuable symptom controls; one of these is mental health, or cognitive fitness.

Bullying and mental health

Just like your body, your cognition follows a predictable pattern of growth and decline over your lifetime. From the moment you are born, your cognitive fitness improves until it plateaus around age twenty-four. It stays around the same until you're fifty and then slowly declines. According to a 2005 study, 50% of mental illness emerges by the age of 14 and 75% by the time we are 24.[9] As with physical fitness, however, your cognitive fitness goes through periodic ups and downs. Some declines are due to simple, acute poor health, like colds and flu. More serious, chronic mental health problems may be associated with your genetic profile and possible predispositions. Your environment, such where you are raised and go to school, then where you live and work, also has an impact. Life events can impact your cognitive fitness

8   X Wang et al, 'Metabolic tuning of inhibition regulates hippocampal neurogenesis in the adult brain', *PNAS*, 41 (12 October 2020), 117, https://doi.org/10.1073/pnas.2006138117, accessed 7 May 2021

9   RC Kessler, P Berglund, O Demler, R Jin, KR Merikangas, EE Walters, 'Lifetime Prevalence and Age-of-Onset Distributions of DSM-IV Disorders in the National Comorbidity Survey Replication', *Archives of General Psychiatry*, 62/6 (2005), 593–602, http://doi.org/10.1001/archpsyc.62.6.593

level: having a baby (which can bring a lack of sleep), going through the menopause and experiencing stress at home or at work. A lot of research has found a correlation between cognitive fitness and socio-economic status, but a report by the Bill and Melinda Gates Foundation showed that mental fitness is a big predictor of academic success and quality of life even when controlling for intelligence quotient (IQ) scores or socio-economic status. This is why we hope that in the not-too-distant future it will be common, from around age six until we die, to regularly test our mental fitness and health, just as we go for regular checkups with our dentist.

Regardless of the many influencing factors, you can always do something to improve your cognitive fitness, whatever your age, gender, socio-economic position, culture or health status. Considering how important our cognition is, are we doing all we can to improve our mental fitness and that of the people we care about? You can test your mental fitness in just fifteen minutes through our clinically validated app, accessible via our website www.notavictim.co.uk. The app tests the five key areas of mental health, or cognitive domains:

1. **Executive function** is the equivalent of your physical core. It connects the other four domains, playing a modulatory role that is crucial in virtually all aspects of cognition. Among other things, it is important for planning and creativity.

2. **Working memory** is the 'workspace' in your mind. It governs your ability to make decisions and solve problems.

3. **Episodic memory** enables the recollection of specific events, situations and experiences.

4. **Processing speed** is the rate and accuracy at which you can carry out different cognitive operations. It enables you to do things without necessarily thinking about the task at hand.

5. **Attention** is the ability to concentrate and focus. Attention involves many interrelated cognitive functions, allowing you to focus on a task even when selectively distracted.

You might be wondering what all this has to do with bullying. Well, if your child's mental fitness is weak, they have a bigger chance of not being able to deal with bullying. Recognising this will help us to mentor them. Knowing that their brains are not yet fully developed, we can adapt how much information we give them, and mentor them accordingly. The app can also show us, objectively, whether our interventions and mentoring are having the desired effects.

Stress vs trauma

'Stress' might be the most used and most misunderstood word in modern times. When people talk about stress, they are often referring to a negative, unnatural feeling. But stress is a normal and natural reaction to an outside event or threat. We need it; it makes us aware that something has changed. Stress is impossible to prevent or stop; without it, we would be in trouble. We can, however, increase our tolerance of perceived threats, so that we have less chance of experiencing prolonged stress. For example, the first time you talk in front of a group of people, it might be stressful, but if you do it often enough, it can feel as normal as walking.

Before we look at stress in more detail, there is a distinction to be made between stress and trauma. We can be stressed without trauma, but trauma cannot occur without stress. With trauma, which is an inappropriate reaction to a stressful event, stress becomes linked to the memory, and so can arise at any moment and cause us to go into defensive or survival mode without any reason or threat.

What exactly happens to our body when we are stressed? Ideally, we would all like to be calm and focused all the time. These states are regulated by our autonomic nervous system, which has three branches, but here we are concerned with only two of them: the sympathetic branch, which makes us alert, and the parasympathetic branch, which makes us calm, for rest and digestion (mental as well as physical).

When we are stressed, the sympathetic branch of our nervous system becomes active, because it wants us to move or do something (this state is also called arousal). It's not as simple as an 'on/off' switch, as there are different levels of stress:

- **Eustress:** The optimal amount of stress for the activity we are undertaking. It's a good type of stress that means when we need to work, we are alert.

- **Hyperstress:** When there is too much arousal, which limits our ability to move and think clearly.

- **Hypostress:** When there is not enough stress, so that we feel tired or lethargic, bored or restless, even depressed.

As we have seen, being alert is useful, but too much alertness is not. If we are in this state, it will be harder for us to focus on things other than self-preservation, and we become less creative and organised. This is far from the ideal state to be in. At school, children are now more cautious than ever, because everything they do can be filmed by other children and with one click can be shared with the world. This can put your child in a constant state of over-alertness, which is draining and unhealthy. The above levels of stress exist on a continuum. We can be in a state of calm alertness, above that a more focused alertness, above that hyperstress, and above that panic. In the other direction, we can go from calm, to tiredness, to lethargy, to depression. Because most people don't consciously control their stress levels, they can spend their whole lives at its mercy. When you add uncertainty to stress, you get fear. Almost all bullying starts in the verbal zone and a lot of it stays there; there is a threat, but in most cases not a direct one. Nevertheless, we perceive it and fear enters our mind. Fear can arise when false evidence or expectations appear real. Thinking will tell us whether the threat is real, whether we are in physical danger or whether our fear is what Michael Gervais calls FOPO: fear of people's opinions, or fear of (our) personal opinions. Or, to interpret the acronym another way: fear of possible outcome, or fear of perceived outcome.

Even though the system is 'autonomic', it is something we can consciously control. In fact, stress operates rather like a thermostat. We can turn it up or down depending on how much we need – if we know how and we practise.

One easy way we can do this is through our breathing. The phrenic nerve passes down the spine between the lungs and heart and controls the diaphragm. This means it can control breathing. If you are agitated or having a panic attack, inhale twice through your nose, then exhale through your mouth. Repeat this three times. As well as being able to calm ourselves through slow, controlled breathing, we can also breathe in a way which will increase our alertness and ability to respond quickly. In the case of bullying, stress is a normal reaction. What we don't want to happen is for this stress to become trauma. The key is to realise that the threat is not real, and so it is a normal reaction but at an inappropriate time.

Andrew Huberman says when something is not being done on automatic pilot, our brain likes to predict three things: duration, path and outcome. In other words, how long it is going to take, how we are going to do it, and what the (desired) outcome is.[10] We have reimagined this as an SOS signal. When something is uncertain, imagine your brain sending out an SOS signal for help, asking you to identify:

- S = stretch (how long it will take to resolve)

- O = outcome (what you want to happen)

- S = strategy (how best to achieve that)

This process can help prevent stress from becoming trauma. We all have bad moments, but it is important to realise that they are only moments. We sometimes say we are having a 'bad day', when in fact we have had only a few bad moments in that day. People suffering from trauma, however, expect those bad moments to recur, even when they are having a good day. To them, those moments feel like something that will last for ever. It's important to bring that person into the present, to show them that they are safe, away from the trauma, and to encourage optimism so that they think of the future as a time when good things

---

10   Whoop, 'Episode 69: Andrew Huberman, Stanford Neuroscientist', The Whoop Podcast (2020), www.whoop.com/thelocker/podcast-69-dr-andrew-huberman-stanford-neuroscientist

will happen. It is a matter of adjusting the thermostat so that we experience stress only when it is needed (during those 'bad' moments) and not when it isn't (the rest of the time).

Our brain processes information through sensation, perception, emotions, thoughts and actions. We often try to respond to negative experiences by first trying to feel better, by telling ourselves to calm down, but this is like mental juggling. What we need is to turn down our stress thermostat.

We must also train ourselves to increase our stress threshold, so that we can stay in uncomfortable states without losing mental clarity, answer the SOS and work out what to do. We should first ensure that general vitality is high, because when our vitality is low our stress threshold also goes down. We should also develop control of our breathing and challenge ourselves more often. This will enable us not only to raise our threshold but also, when we reach that threshold, to recover more quickly.

Our task is to break the link between the stressful event (bullying) and the future (trauma). This is an incremental process, which is another reason why it's so important to mentor our child, because it's easier to prevent the problems from occurring than to fix them after they do. As children, we lay the foundations that we will use as adults; we don't suddenly start using different pathways in our brains when we turn eighteen.

It is important to realise that trauma can result from even a small, seemingly insignificant event, such as Menno's experience of wetting himself at school, which we discuss later. This was a non-threatening situation but became the source of an obsessive-compulsive disorder that lasted for ten years.

We need to learn how to deal with stress, anxiety and fear in the same way that we deal with hunger or thirst. The SOS process can help us. Particularly important is the first S (stretch, or duration). Stress often changes our perception of time. Stressful events feel as if they are lasting longer than they are, lowering our tolerance for discomfort. If you are told that you'll experience the most terrifying pain you have ever felt, but only for one second, you can prepare for it; you might think, 'I can take that.' But if you don't know how long the pain will last, your reaction will be completely different.

The first S is about getting perspective, about reducing the challenge to something that is manageable. This is achieved by recognising our ability to control our actions, thoughts and internal states in the present and taking small incremental steps to deal with the issue we're facing.

It's important to remind yourself that stress will happen; it's a normal reaction in life. But we must try not to stress about things that aren't happening and aren't likely to happen, to not stay in the stress zone longer than necessary.

Understanding how stress and trauma work will put you in a better position to mentor your child to read and regulate their own state, depending on what is necessary, to prevent present stress becoming future trauma.

The missing F

People often talk about the freeze, flight, fight and fright stress responses that we choose from when we are (or at least, we think we are) in danger. Our senses are heightened, and our autonomic nervous system is activated, in the interest of survival. People tend to react in the same way to stress – you can't stop the fright stress response – it is automatic so happens quickly and unconsciously. What happens next often depends on people's training and values. The people who we interviewed that were bullied said most of the time they froze or fled. When we asked them to imagine what they would do if a loved one was in the same situation, they all said they would stay to confront the threat and stand up for that person. Our tendency is not to confront a threat or challenge, but to run away or freeze. This is because our default mode is pessimism, not optimism. Optimism is a trained skill,[11] and so is fighting.

Understanding this, we see why it is essential to prepare our child for encountering external threats.

---

11 Brian Mackenzie, Interview with Michael Gervais at 09:36 (30 June 2020), www.instagram.com/p/CCENsTnltjh, accessed 7 May 2021

Otherwise, we may be setting them on the path to becoming a victim. There is another F response that is not so well known, which is flow. Flow is the optimal state a human being can be in. When we have flow, we feel and perform at our best. The happiest people in the world are those with the most flow.

Flow is not a state which comes and goes; it can be trained, and this is an important skill for your child to acquire. It has nothing to do with the common notion that life should be easy all the time, or that you should just 'go with the flow'. Flow is not an off/on switch but a four-phase cycle, FLFL, consisting of:

1. **Frustration:** Where you struggle with a challenge that is greater than your skillset, the magic formula being that the challenge should exceed your skillset by 4% (if it's too much bigger, you can become anxious; not enough, and there is no challenge).

2. **Letting go:** Where you take your mind off the struggle and wash away the stress hormones from the first phase.

3. **Flow:** Where you and the activity merge as one and time either slows down or goes by quickly; your inner critic is silenced, and things feel effortless. You often gain great insights, and magic happens.

4. **Loading:** The recovery phase, where you either unload (discharge) and then reload/recharge

yourself and upload what you have learned for the next cycle of flow, so that what was possible only during flow, through practice, becomes possible outside of it.

There can't be flow without frustration and a struggle. To progress, we need to push our capabilities. When your child is confronted by a bully, there will be stress and a struggle. These feelings and impulses must be confronted if your child is to develop their skills. They must learn to confront their fear and 'fight back socially', not freeze or flee. Fighting back socially means learning to stand up for yourself verbally, refusing to be submissive in a bullying situation and doing your best to prevent escalation to physical confrontation so these incidences stop re-occurring in the future.

Georges St-Pierre is generally regarded as one of the best martial artists in the world. He was bullied as a child but later became a two-time UFC World Champion. He doesn't hide the fact that he is terrified before every fight. When you look at him before he walks into the ring, he looks confident, but deep down inside he is scared as hell. He doesn't run from his emotions, he embraces them; the closer he gets to the ring, the more confident he gets.

3
Breaking Bullying Down

People who don't do martial arts often look at black belts in awe, thinking they must be bulletproof. But this is not the case. Martial artists simply learn what to do if someone attacks them. They are prepared for getting hit, so when things get heated, they know they won't panic but will act as they have been trained to. If you assume you won't get hit or hurt, you will struggle to deal with it if you do.

The truths of bullying

We have distilled our knowledge and experience of bullying into 'bullying truths':

1. Bullying is part of the human condition

We see it all the time: people and organisations want to eradicate bullying, just as they want to eradicate disease, loneliness, fear or anxiety. The fact is, bullying will always occur. It's not easy, but nor is life. Avoidance only increases your chance of experiencing bullying; building resilience is fundamental.

2. The bullied must change before the bully

We must teach our child to love what makes them, them, as this can't be changed, but could make them a target for a bully. For instance, if they are incredibly tall, you could encourage them to play basketball; then, if people make fun of them for being tall, they won't care because they would feel empowered by that characteristic. By learning to adapt, the one who is bullied becomes stronger than the bully.

3. Bullying impacts the whole family

When a child is being bullied and isn't coping with it, it can affect all areas of their life. This is why this book is so important, as it will teach you how to enable your child to cope with bullying.

4. Bullying will cause emotional triggers to resurface

Bullying is such a sensitive, emotional topic that it will cause previous emotional triggers or trauma in parents to resurface, which will shape how you respond and mentor your child – for better or worse.

5. Bullying is predictable

If they are bullied, there are two possible three-stage paths your child will follow, three moments of magic or misery. You can plan for both.

Experiencing bullying increases the risk of bullying others This is why understanding bullying, why it occurs and how to deal with, and deconstructing the bully–victim relationship is vital.

6. Bullying is a transition, not a one-off event

We should perhaps recognise that bullying in our lives can be positive as it helps us to learn about conflict and confrontation and understand how to manage difficult social situations. When you remove your child from this experience, it will resurface, and the cycle can repeat into adulthood.

7. Your child will either break, through bullying, or break through bullying

Bullying has the power to make or break their character, so how they are mentored through this transition will affect how they live the rest of their life.

8. Bullying can be a positive force

Interviewing dozens of successful people who have gone through bullying and attributed a large part of their success to this experience has convinced us that bullying can be a positive driving force, providing it is put in the right context and appropriate mentorship is received.

9. Most parents are reactive, not proactive

Most parents respond to bullying reactively. They don't expect their child to be bullied, so they wait until they are and then try to do something about it. Invariably, their judgement in this situation is poor and their reaction is badly managed. This is why we stress the importance of preparation.

10. Your child might not tell you they are being bullied

You can have the best relationship in the world with your child, it is still likely that they won't tell you they are being bullied, perhaps for years.

11. The trauma of bullying is not linked to the severity of bullying...

... but to your child's ability to feel, heal and deal with it. Some people think that a little bullying won't do any harm, but it can be damaging if your child doesn't know how to handle it.

12. There is no difference between teasing and bullying

People often think that teasing is okay. 'I was just teasing', they will say. But they forget that their intention doesn't predict the hurt that is caused, which will depend on the tolerance of the person on the receiving end.

13. You can't prevent bullying altogether

People are creative; they can bully someone for any reason under the sun. They can bully you for being yourself; they can bully you for not being yourself. Just as you protect your loved ones when they are under attack, you must learn to protect yourself too.

14. You can't break through bullying for your child

We want to protect our child, but we can't and won't always be there for them. You might want to solve the bullying for them because the challenge seems too big for them at that moment. This doesn't equip your child with the resilience and principles they will need to overcome similar obstacles in the future.

15. Bullying can help your child to develop

If we are learning the piano, we practise until we get it right, and then practise some more until we can't get it wrong. The same applies to bullying; dealing with it requires practice.

16. Words don't hurt; you let words hurt you

Words can only impact you if you let them. Think about it, if someone called you names in a foreign language, would it have the same effect as if they had said the same thing in your language?

17. We all need a safe word

This is about making time for the child you love. You need a word that tells you that your child is in need of your help, now. This is the magic button we discussed earlier.

18. The bully is a victim

Happy children don't bully. The bully is a victim trying desperately to handle a situation or state that is beyond their control. Your child has the chance to enable their bully to break the cycle of bullying and set them up for a successful life.

19. We all need a safe environment

Every child needs a safe environment, a place where they can be themselves, where they can challenge themselves, a place they look forward to being in.

Different types of bullying

When we talk about bullying, most people think about physical bullying, but there are several other types of bullying, such as mental and/or emotional bullying, which includes cyberbullying (the subject of the next section); and self-bullying, both mental and physical. Life itself can also be a kind of bully. We all have to deal with challenges in our lives, but if we haven't learned how to overcome them, these challenges can have a similar effect to a bully.

We tend to focus on bullies as other people, and rarely on us bullying ourselves. But being bullied by someone else can cause your child to start bullying themselves. If the bully keeps repeating an image of your child that is different from the one they have of themselves, their self-image can start to change. In fact, that's often why kids become bullies, because they don't feel good themselves. Even when the bullying has stopped, this negative image can persist, sometimes for the rest of their life. While we are teaching our child about bullying, we should teach them about self-bullying so that, if it happens, they can recognise it without judgement and be in a better state to deal with it.

This is illustrated by Menno's personal experience:

MENNO'S STORY

When I was eleven years old and in the last class of elementary school, I suddenly needed to go to the toilet. I had already been earlier that morning, but I had to go again, urgently. I raised my hand and asked for permission, but I wasn't allowed to go. I tried to focus on the work I had to do, but I couldn't hold it and I wet myself as I ran out of the classroom.

Although I was neither punished nor bullied as a result, I was ashamed of what had happened and became terrified of wetting myself again at school. As I walked to school, I would hope it wouldn't happen, and throughout the school day I would think about it.

This anxiety continued at high school, even though I had the opportunity to go to the toilet before every lesson. I couldn't focus on my schoolwork. Worse, because I was so focused on this anxiety, my mind created urges to pee, which felt real but weren't. I would even go to the toilet and be unable to pee. To resist the urges or push them away, I constantly pressed on my lower belly. This made me feel that I was the centre of everyone's attention; I felt ashamed and insecure.

After high school, I studied physical therapy for four years. The first two years, I continued my destructive habit of being scared before classes, continuously going to the toilet and worrying about not wetting myself during class. It was not until my third year of the course that I finally broke these habits.

Over a period of a decade, I must have thought about not wetting myself at least twenty times a day, five days a week, for forty weeks a year: a total of 40,000 stressful thoughts. I had allowed a single event when I was eleven to become a major trauma.

My parents didn't know about any of this until I told them when I was in my twenties. I don't know why I didn't ask them for help at the time, but I wish I had; it would have saved me ten years of pain and I likely would have done better at school.

If something like this happens to your child, don't try to make it smaller or wave it away. Think how their brain will handle it. They don't have a strategy to cope with what has happened and recover from it.

We teach our kids how to protect themselves against physical dangers, from crossing the road to talking to strangers. We must also teach them how to protect themselves against non-physical threats, both external and internal.

Self-bullying can become physical, not just in direct self-harming but in indirect ways, where the child doesn't take care of their body, of their physical and mental health, so that their vitality slowly declines, which puts them at a greater risk of physical injury, disease and mental illness. The decline can be so slow that it goes unnoticed for years before effects emerge.

Cyberbullying

A particular type of bullying that has become increasingly prevalent in recent years is cyberbullying, and we could find no one better to talk about it than Barry Lee Cummings, one of the world's leading cybersafety experts. We asked him to explain what cyberbullying is and why it is so difficult to deal with.

CYBERBULLYING – AN INTERVIEW WITH BARRY LEE CUMMINGS

What is cyberbullying?

Cyberbullying manifests in a variety of forms, but its official definition is 'the use of technology to repeatedly and intentionally harass, hurt, embarrass, humiliate, or intimidate another person.'[12]

The reality is that this is occurring more and more to and by young people. To the point where in a recent poll I ran with more than 1,800 students, over 50% of tweens and teenagers said they thought cyberbullying was just a part of growing up and therefore normal.[13] While I subscribe to the notion that this is unfortunately something most young people are going to have to deal with, I refuse to agree that this is 'normal'. It most certainly isn't and the course can be changed with education and awareness around digital self-defence.

Outside of the playground, cyberbullying is a rapidly rising problem because a bully can hide behind a computer screen, give themselves a new name and be virtually undetectable. Anonymity is one of the big factors in the growth of cyberbullying.

How is cyberbullying different from 'traditional' forms of bullying?

It's often an extension of traditional bullying, but really, we are dealing with a different enemy altogether here – one that requires a different approach. If your child is being bullied in person, for example in the playground, removing them from the situation immediately stops this from occurring.

Today, our children have access to phones, computers, iPads etc and as parents we don't know what is going on online. Bullying is even harder to spot. Your child's

12   Pacer's National Bullying Prevention Center, www.pacer.org/
     bullying/info/cyberbullying, accessed 7 May 2021
13   Beat The Cyberbully 2019 (online poll carried out by Barry Lee
     Cummings and his team)

bullying may not be occurring locally, but globally. With public profiles, we open the door to everyone, without limit. Children who lack supervision or feel like prisoners in their own home are even more susceptible to cyberbullying.

Does cyberbullying pose a greater threat to young people than 'traditional' bullying?

I believe it does. And, as it stands, it's relatively unresearched. Technology is developing so quickly that it's hard for us to look back, gather evidence and compare, before a new app, a new platform, software or social media tool comes out and a new way to cyberbully emerges. How can we embrace technology and all of its benefits while also protecting our children? Answering this raises a lot of other questions. First, how can we keep on top of all the changes, with new apps, games, software and social media platforms posing new threats every week? Is it enough to restrict children in their use of social media, or is there a better way to protect them? What is the best way to open the conversation with young people on the topic of cyberbullying? After all, to a teenager the threat of having their WiFi removed can feel like a life-or-death situation.

To begin with, there's the issue of 'digital diligence'. What we mean here is when children and young people are given tools that provide access to the digital space with little to no guidance as to how to use them. It's not a deliberate lack of digital diligence, it's usually more a lack of understanding or awareness on behalf of parents and carers in terms of what they are actually doing when they think they are making their children happy by saying yes to their request for a new smartphone for a birthday, a tablet for Christmas or a gaming console for getting good grades.

I don't know many parents who would hand their ten-year-old a chainsaw and tell them to go out into the garden and 'play'. And yet many of us hand over smart devices to our child and leave them to figure it out for themselves. Both tools have the potential to create massive harm, but we don't put them in the same category of danger. Of course, our child knows this and will use it against us.

As a society, we are in a transitional period where there isn't one party – parent, child or young person – who knows exactly what's going on when it comes to growing up in a digital age. We have a generation of parents – classified as Boomers, Generation X and Xennials – who didn't go through their tween and teen years with the digital layer, trying to bring up their Millennials and Generation Zers without a road map. Unable to fall back on how they were brought up, parents are having to create their own road map, but they are having to do it on the fly, in real time.

This doesn't absolve us, as parents, of our responsibilities. We need to develop the resources that our children want, need and deserve, which means increasing our knowledge of the world they live in, upgrading our awareness of the pitfalls of the digital space.

To begin with, and to put cyberbullying in its proper perspective, we must understand that our children's online safety and ability to protect themselves goes way beyond cyberbullying. There are all kinds of top-ics we have to decide how to speak to our children about, including some unpleasant ones that we may not want to discuss with them. But if we don't, they are going to learn about these subjects from their peers, Instagram or YouTube, for example, places that I think you would agree are not where you want your children getting certain parts of their education from.

As parents, our child's safety in the digital space must be near the top of our priority list. Whether we like it or not, this is their world, and they are going to be spending a lot of time in it during their formative years. First of all, this means constant education for us as parents. We recognise that this is a massive chal-lenge, but it is one that we need to face if we are to keep our child safe.

One thing we can do is establish acceptable use poli-cies (AUPs). These are usually provided by compa-nies to employees to control things like social media use at work, but AUPs are also essential in the home, in particular to keep internet use in check. Here are the six factors to consider when developing an AUP:

1. **Collaboration:** It's essential that you and your child build the AUP together. This increases the likelihood of acceptance and compliance.

2. **Commitment:** Everyone must commit to the AUP; it must be applicable to the whole family, not just your child.

3. **Flexibility:** Acknowledge that the AUP is going to change. It isn't set in stone and will be amended as platforms change, as technology moves on and, of course, as your child gets older.

4. **Clarity:** There must be no room for confusion. This prevents the 'Oh, I didn't think you meant that' excuse when the rules are broken.

5. **Transparency:** Everyone must be open and honest about their internet use, and aware of the reasons for any parental control software that is installed.[14]

6. **Sanctions:** There must be clear sanctions for breaking rules, and these must be imposed without exception; otherwise, there is no incentive to obey them. This is where a lot of AUPs fall down.

Your AUPs should include a 'no devices in bedrooms at night' rule and parental approval for all app downloads (both Apple and Google have family account set-ups that enable this).

Beyond that, your child needs to be encouraged to think about what they are putting out through digital channels to ensure that their 'digital tattoo' is true a reflection of the way they want people to see them. The idea of online reputation is something that can

---

14 We recommend the following parental control software: Boomerang, Circle, iKydz, Nischint.

be introduced to children as young as ten; we must reinforce the idea that *everything* you put online, stays online.

Our children are believing the claims of 'disappearing content' and thinking they don't have to worry about what they put out there because it's temporary, but that's simply not true. Everything you put online leaves a trail, and in 99% of cases it stays online forever – even if you delete it or an app tells you that it's gone after ten seconds. This is why we call it a digital tattoo – it's permanent and goes with you everywhere.

Online grooming

Online grooming, which is unfortunately prevalent, is the process whereby a predator looks to establish an online relationship with a child or young person and build up their trust in that relationship to a point where requests to meet in the real world, or the sending of sexual images or videos, are viewed as acceptable. In the latter case, this can lead to demands for money (extortion) with the threat of sharing the images/videos with family, friends, school year groups and so on. This is a horrible situation for anyone to find themselves in, let alone a child. Grooming can have truly tragic consequences, as the following story illustrates.

BRECK BEDNAR

Breck was groomed online through his gaming console, in full view of his friends and his mum. The groomer was playing a long game; it took time to gain Breck's trust and start to create a distance between him and his mum to the point where one day, instead of going to visit his dad in London as had been planned, he took himself to his new friend's flat, where he was abused, assaulted and murdered.

What compounds the tragedy is that Breck's mum was heavily involved in his digital life and had noticed changes in behaviour but was still powerless to stop the advances of the killer, who would even tell Breck to, 'Say hello' to her when he knew she was around. Suspecting that he was being groomed, she went to the police, but nothing was done about it. It took the tragic loss of his life for the police to reform the way they handled such cases.

Unfortunately, the way in which children use the internet and its platforms provides predators such as Breck's killer with a much larger pool of opportunity.

Breck's story has been turned into a docudrama entitled *Murder Games: The Life and Death of Breck Bednar*,[15] and his mother has sought to use the tragic loss of her son as a motivation for other parents and caregivers to understand what their children are doing in the online space.

---

15 *Murder Games: The Life and Death of Breck Bednar* (BBC, 2018)

So, is it a matter of educating our child on the dangers of cyberspace? The reality of the digital world we live in is that, unfortunately, it's almost guaranteed that our child will be exposed to cyberbullying at some point. This means that we have to help them build resilience by equipping them with the tools to recognise what is happening and overcome it, whatever form it takes.

The most effective way of doing this is through open communication channels between children and parents. But this is hard to do when we parents may feel we have no commonality with them, and our child thinks that we don't know anything about their world.

This is where the work begins for many of us. As early as possible, we have to find ways to talk our child's language, which means finding an interest in things that perhaps wouldn't interest us. If we take the time to foster and cultivate that interest, we can empower our children to view cyberbullying a different way.

Our final story on cyberbullying shows how this can be achieved.

KEHKASHAN BASU

Kehkashan and her family are a great example of how the family unit can help overcome cyberbullying and thrive in spite of it. Kehkashan was cyberbullied from age eight, when she began to receive negative content aimed at her and her family, including death threats.

From a young age, she had wanted to make a difference and knew that in order to do so, leveraging the tools at her disposal, the internet, would be key. At age twelve she founded an organisation called Green Hope, a global youth enterprise to promote sustainable development. This was part of the reason for some of the cyberbullying.

She wasn't prepared for the hatred and vitriol that accompanied putting herself out there to do good, but her parents taught her to flip the narrative and to understand that what was being aimed at her was not a reflection of her, but a reflection of those that were cyberbullying – that they were voicing the things that they were most unhappy about in themselves.

By age twenty, as a student at the University of Toronto, Kehkashan had turned Green Hope into an international organisation making an impact in countries all over the world. She has been ranked one of Canada's top 100 most powerful women and been included in the ForbesUnder30 list for her work on education for sustainable development, among many accolades.

Kehkashan is still cyberbullied to this day, but she falls back on her learning as a twelve-year-old, that really, it's all about the bully's own issues.[16]

---

16 World Future Council, 'Kehkashan Basu' (no date), www. worldfuturecouncil. org/p/kehkashan-basu, accessed 2 June 2021; Kids Rights, '2016 – Kehkashan Basu (16), UAE' (2016), https://kidsrights.org/advocacy/international-childrens-peace-prize/winners/kehkashan-basu, accessed 2 June 2021; Beat the cyberbully, 'Beat the cyberbully makes TV debut in UAE', Blog (2014), https://beatthecyberbully.ae/beat-they-cyberbully-makes-tv-debut-in-uae, accessed 13 June 2021

Some final words of advice for parents and children on dealing with cyberbullying. First, from the child's point of view, Kehkashan's advice to anyone that is going through cyberbullying, or knows someone who is: speak to someone, speak up and don't suffer alone. You are not on your own and together you can overcome just about any obstacle.

For parents, we would add: be aware, be informed, be a part of the conversation – at family level, school level, community level and at societal level. By being involved in your child's digital life from an informed perspective you can guide and protect them more effectively.

4
The Effects Of Bullying

We have worked with over 5,000 families and this has given us incredible insights into the challenges parents face, raising their children from the age of four to eighteen. In the last two years, we have interviewed more than 2,000 parents and have found that three transitions that a child goes through keep coming up in our conversations. These transitions impact the whole family, not just the child, and are the root of many challenges that children face. These transitions typically (although not always) happen in the following order:

1. Changing schools

2. Adolescence

3. Separation and loss

We will look at each of these three transitions in detail to give you an insight into why they are so important for your child.

Changing schools

The most common difficult transition young people make is from primary to secondary school, between the ages of ten and twelve. This is a crucial time. As a child's immediate community suddenly changes, their friendships also change and they have to quickly create new friendships in a harsher social environment – where they have gone from being the oldest, to the youngest – in order to fit in and prevent isolation. On top of this, there is increased pressure from a more demanding academic schedule. A huge amount of benefit can come from having a sustained community like a club or activity where they feel at home, respected and happy at this stage.

A common mistake we find parents making is to take their child out of any club they've been attending as they go through this transition in the hope that they will make new friends and take up new clubs or opportunities in their new school. This is a mistake for three main reasons:

1. It's a gamble that the child will make friends quickly and not be isolated in their new school.

They might not fit in perfectly to one of the new clubs they have the option to join.

2. They might have worked hard to build a strong sense of community in their current club. Taking this away from them at the same time as losing the community of their primary school can be too much of a shock. Consistency in daily or weekly routines (like going to a particular class) can do wonders for maintaining and improving confidence.

3. The benefits of a strong community are built up over many years, so they have a powerful cumulative effect if a child stays in that community. They can teach the new skills they possess to others, and this leadership has a profound effect on their sense of self, their sense of pride and the development of their character.

To gain a deeper understanding of bullying we must first have a deep understanding of the difficult times a child may face, which can often be a perfect time for bullying to occur. When a child's community or emotional state is disrupted, they are far more likely to be targeted and experience bullying.

Adolescence

This biological transition shakes the emotional foundations of almost every young person as they develop.

This is also a time that parents dread, as their brilliant children can become argumentative, irrational, aggressive, hyper-sensitive, unhappy and difficult to live with. Puberty strikes, hormones erupt like a volcano, girlfriends or boyfriends arrive on the scene (with all the emotions they bring) and all rationality goes out of the window.

The journal *Psychology Today* characterises adolescence in the following way:

'This transitional period can bring up issues of independence and self-identity; many adolescents and their peers face tough choices regarding schoolwork, sexuality, drugs, alcohol, and social life. Peer groups, romantic interests, and appearance tend to naturally increase in importance for some time during a teen's journey towards adulthood.'[17]

Usually, adolescence is the period between the ages of thirteen and nineteen, the time when a child turns into an adult. The physical and psychological changes often begin earlier, though, during the preteen or 'tween' years (ages nine to twelve).

Cognitive fitness, emotional intelligence (a high emotional IQ) and a sense of self-worth all have a stabilising effect on the strong emotions of adolescence. Your child's emotional IQ is a measure of their empathy.

---

17 'Adolescence', *Psychology Today* (no date), www.psychologytoday. com/us/basics/adolescence, accessed 8 May 2021

This can be developed by encouraging them to think about the effects of their actions on others and to always behave with courtesy and respect towards others. By prioritising these values as a means to control our behaviour, we strengthen and increase their executive function and consequently our emotional IQ. A higher emotional IQ will mean your child has better judgement about how to behave or, if they have behaved poorly, will help them analyse their behaviour and its negative effect on others. This results in less sulking, less self-isolation in the bedroom, more apologies and faster repairing of relationships.

Many of the problems we've observed in adolescence centre around self-worth; these can last many years. It's at this time that young people are trying to find their place and get a grasp of who they are and what they are worth. With a negative inner critic and poorly developed self-esteem or self-image, this time can be damaging. A supportive community can identify weak areas, help young people take big steps to improve them and provide emotional support. All this gives young people the protective kit to weather the storm of adolescence and come out well developed and ready for adulthood.

There is much benefit to be gained during this challenging time. A young person asks themselves so many meaningful questions during adolescence and, with the right mentoring and support network, this provides a huge opportunity for introspective enlightenment.

Separation and loss

Though not as common as the other two transitions, which almost every child will go through, separation or loss is a major transition most children must go through. By separation, we are referring to the separation of the child's parents, which inevitably involves the partial (and sometimes complete) separation of the child from one or other parent.

Loss can apply to the child's parents as well as the child themselves, and can be any of the following:

- Loss of a parent or parents
- Loss of brothers/sisters
- Loss of a child
- Loss of friends
- Loss of love
- Loss of a limb
- Loss of a physical function
- Loss of work
- Loss of enjoyment of a hobby
- Loss of business
- Loss of money

We have had the privilege of working with some incredible single parents who lived for many years in a toxic relationship, doing their best to raise their children in a harmful environment. Their children blossomed once a change occurred. In these cases, the separation benefitted the child's development. We've also seen children watch their parents separate, which has caused huge emotional disruption – to their mental health, social situation and immediate community – and resulted in poor behaviour, lowered confidence, a lack of focus, increased risk of bullying and difficulty trusting people in authority.

The one undeniable truth we have discovered is that whether or not separation or loss is damaging depends on how the parents process the change for their child. When jealousy, manipulation and negative remarks play a role, the damage can be huge. Our children learn about relationships by watching us and this learned behaviour often manifests in their own lives. If parents have made the decision to divorce or separate and they are able to put their child first, remaining entirely positive, explaining the situation in a loving and caring way without diminishing the roles of the mother and father and maintaining the strong bonds they have with their child, this will minimise the disruption.

If your child is currently experiencing bullying, ask yourself if they are going through any of these transitions. Often, a child who is being bullied is experiencing two or even all three transitions at the same time. A sudden change in your child's emotional stability and in their immediate community can be the catalyst for bullying. We have seen, for example, a child starting to go through severe bullying after the family had experienced financial trouble.

You may have noticed that we call these challenges transitions and not events. This is because typically they involve a series of events over a period of time, rather than a single moment. We can define a transition as a process or a period of changing from one state or condition to another. In this sense, bullying, too, is a transition. This book (and our work in general) is about how to mentor your child through the transition of bullying so that they come out a happy and successful adult. You cannot do this if you are unaware that your child is being bullied. The terrifying thing for parents is that bullying often occurs without their knowing. If, as is often the case, your child doesn't tell you they are being bullied, you need to be able to recognise the tell-tale signs.

Ten signs your child is being bullied

One of the biggest problems we have found in our work with families, which is echoed in the feedback from the thousands of interviews we have carried out with parents, is that it's rarely obvious that your child is being bullied. Often, the subtle changes that occur go under the radar. The trouble is that when we do finally discover that our child is being bullied, they have already been experiencing it for a long time. While bullying is a transition and a learning opportunity that a child can grow from, they need us to implement practical steps and mentoring right from the start (and even beforehand) to help them get through this transition quickly.

Based on our experience, these are the ten most common signs to watch out for:

1. Your child is depressed

Children who go through bullying often show insecurity, depression, loneliness and low self-esteem. They may say they are tired and want to sleep more or stop enjoying activities they previously got a lot of joy from.

2. Your child has aggressive outbursts at home

When a child is going through bullying, their emotions can build up over time and outbursts are likely. They act in this way because they feel comfortable showing their emotions at home. This is a clear sign of built-up tension.

3. Your child doesn't want to go to school or a club/ class

If your child suddenly shows a lack of interest in school or their clubs / classes, this may be an indication of bullying. They may want to avoid school entirely because they know they are likely to be bullied.

4. Your child's behaviour gets worse or their grades go down

If your child is typically well behaved but you start to receive reports of bad behaviour, or if their grades inexplicably decline, this can be a clear sign that they are being bullied.

5. Your child has unexplained injuries

When bullying becomes severe, it can turn physical. If your child is displaying (or trying to hide) injuries or bruises, this is a sign of bullying. Don't be tempted to brush this aside, thinking 'kids will be kids'. Make a note of any injuries and see if a pattern emerges.

6. Your child's self-talk is negative

When you talk to your child about their day, how do they speak about themselves? Can you observe any negative self-talk? How do they analyse their performance? One of the saddest things about bullying is that we often listen to the bullies, accepting their negative comments about us without challenging them and, after a while, come to believe them. Their comments become our thoughts. By listening carefully to your child's self-talk, you will have a good indication of if they are being bullied.

7. Your child self-harms or talks about suicide

Sadly, we have had dealings with dozens of children, especially adolescents, where the subject of self-harming or references to suicide come up in conversation or in their diaries or social media comments. It's vital that this is taken seriously. If it is a sign of bullying, removing your child from the harmful social situation is the most important immediate step. However, teaching them to overcome these challenges is equally important so that it does not repeat in the new social circle.

8. Your child prefers to be alone

If your child suddenly prefers to be alone, this may be an indication that they are being bullied. If we are constantly picked on in a social setting, we will find comfort in our own space. Note that this self-isolation can occur at school rather than at home, eg by hiding in the library during lunch breaks, so it is important to communicate with teachers and school staff as well as observe what is happening at home.

9. Your child's eating habits change

If your child's eating habits change, this could be a psychosomatic response to stress. Stress impacts our appetite. If you notice this and it continues for a prolonged period, look carefully for other signs and open up a dialogue around bullying with your child.

10. Your child starts shying away from challenges

If your child is reluctant to try new things or push themselves to go further in one of their existing activities, or if their progress in a particular activity slows down, this could be another sign that they are being bullied.

Three impacts of bullying

The impacts of bullying manifest in many areas of life, including the decisions we make, how we form relationships and trust one another, the goals and visions we set ourselves and even the way in which we mentor our children. We commonly see three impacts of bullying. Understanding these better will not only help you to recognise when bullying is happening, but also give you direction on how to help your child build skills to deal with it. To remember these three common impacts, we use the acronym RISC.

R = Resilience

As parents, we want our child to grow up to be resilient and self-reliant. But bullying can have the opposite effect, of making your child dependent. There can't be progress without challenges. This is important for both you and your child, because if you consistently do things that your child can do for themselves, they will end up dependent on you, or others. We also see children becoming too reliant on sports/

hobbies or drugs, alcohol or pornography. Our role as parents is to become obsolete. This might not feel nice, but you want your child to be able to stand on their own feet. To progress, you child must learn how to tackle and overcome the challenges that come their way, including bullying. What we notice with some adults who have been bullied as children is that they have huge drive and ambition, but this is accompanied by perfectionism. They think they have to do something in a certain way, or they will not be 'good enough'. We also see it going the other way, where adults avoid challenges altogether. Both are trying to play it safe, and in each case, it limits what they are capable of. More importantly, it prevents them from feeling fully alive in the here and now. They have 'destination addiction' – a preoccupation with the idea that happiness and self-worth are to be achieved in some other place or time. They are reliant on a certain result, either the result of their work or the result of staying safe without progress, which makes them progressively less resilient.

I = Image

We are referring here to both the image your child has of themselves and the image others have of them. As we have seen, bullying can have a damaging effect on self-image. From the bully's point of view, harming your child's self-image makes them an easier target. From your child's point of view, a damaged self-image can put them into a self-imposed prison, from which they believe there is no escape. This can happen if they prioritise others' opinions over their own. It's important to understand that there is only one source of self-confidence, and that is how we talk about and treat ourselves. We want our children to have a positive image of themselves and to do things that can reinforce this. We don't want them to get a false sense of confidence, without the skills and knowledge to back it up, but a genuine sense of self-worth.

SC = Self-control

As we have seen, when a child is being bullied, they often have a hard time controlling their emotions. This may result in them avoiding situations in which they cannot control themselves, or in losing control in what should be manageable situations. This means that we, as mentors, have two responsibilities: to build our child's skill at recognising situations where they won't be able to control themselves, and to develop their ability to control their emotions if they do find themselves in such a situation.

All these three impacts – on resilience, self-control and self-image – can lead to children not living fully or even, sadly, to wanting to stop living altogether. They can also turn your child into a bully, of themselves or others, which will continue the cycle of bullying.

We want to get to a place where our child is **reliant** on themselves to face challenges so that they keep progressing; has a positive, but not delusional, **image** of themselves and the world; and knows how to read situations and exercise **self-control**.

Moments of magic and misery

In our work, we've noticed that students experience three key moments when they go through the difficult transition of bullying. There are three positive moments and three negative moments. Which set of moments they experience is determined by the mentoring they receive and the route they take as they transition through bullying.

Let's explore the three positive moments – what we like to call the 'magical moments' – first:

Awareness

There comes a point when parents and children become aware of the intricacies of bullying, why it occurs and the impacts it can have, and they develop a plan to overcome this difficult transition together. There's a sense of hope, support and positivity. There is light at the end of the tunnel; they can see the horizon again. We often refer to this as a sunrise moment. From the moment of awareness, the process of putting together a plan typically takes two to six weeks of consistent effort.

Breakthrough point

Then there is a moment when the child makes the decision to reject oppression, negativity and injustice, and relinquishes the victim mentality. They decide to stand up for themselves – verbally, physically, even subconsciously – and chooses to live life on their own terms. This decision will be something they reflect on for the rest of their life as the moment of change.

Something we have noticed is that without this decisive moment the child has very little with which to 'frame' their bullying, and they struggle to pivot and progress to the third moment. The bullying often continues into their new social groups and sometimes into adulthood.

Victory: Post-traumatic growth

For many children, bullying is a trauma – the biggest trauma they will ever experience. But, as we have seen, if handled correctly, trauma can result in post-traumatic growth. This typically manifests itself in three areas of a person's life:

- Their emotional intelligence
- Their perspective on life and level of gratitude
- The relationships they form and develop

With a new-found community, or a new-found place in their existing social circle, comes growth in emotional intelligence and self-confidence. It's important to capitalise on this powerful stage by putting in place a character development programme that prevents your child from becoming a bully themselves, and specifically aims to develop their confidence, conduct and concentration.

On the other hand, if a child is not mentored properly through the difficult transition of bullying, they will experience three negative moments – what we call the 'misery moments':

Loss of freedom: Imprisonment

When your child is reluctant to face challenges, avoids going out and meeting people, and prefers to be alone, they can end up feeling like a prisoner in their own home. Or worse, in their own body and mind. We often refer to this as a sunset moment, when your child's horizon disappears from view, their world gets dark, and it becomes harder and harder to see a way out.

A huge part of this misery moment is a breakdown in communication, as your child avoids talking to you about what they are going through – a subject we will be returning to in Part Two.

Breaking point

Your child feels as if a dam is breaking and all the water behind it is crashing down on them. They feel overwhelmed and powerless. They don't know what to do to get through this difficult transition. It all becomes too much to handle and they want to give up. Your child may lash out or erupt. It's often in this moment that the bullying can stop, because your child finally stands up to it. Alternatively, this moment of emotional overload can result in more bullying, as your child is picked on for their 'unacceptable' reaction.

Victim mentality

In this book, we do not talk about your child being a 'victim'. Rather, we stress the importance of implanting the idea in their mind that they are not a victim, that they can overcome bullying. However, without the necessary mentoring and with the first two misery moments behind them, your child is likely to live up to their perceived role of victim.

The moment when a person arrives at a victim mentality is the moment where post-traumatic stress takes the place of post-traumatic growth. This will affect all areas of your child's life – in both the present and the future. At this point, your child will experience one of two outcomes:

Outcome one: A victim mindset. Their body language reveals nervousness and anxiety, their inner thoughts become incredibly negative. They avoid social settings, challenges, adventure and leaving their comfort zone. A victim mindset brings with it a scarcity mindset – that they have a lack of not being enough, or are losing, something. Their growth is drastically limited and, if not addressed, the damage done can last decades and result in chronic stress. Your child's negative experiences will impact how they raise their own children.

Outcome two: Bullying behaviour. If your child stands up to their bullies but is still experiencing post-traumatic stress without the correct mentoring to handle the transition through these emotions, they may find that they enjoy this new feeling of power and become a bully themselves. One of the most shocking discoveries we made while developing our Not A Victim process was that a child who has been bullied is far more likely to become a bully than a child who has not. This was shown by a 2016 study of children in America aged ten to seventeen undertaken by the American Academy of Pediatrics.[18] This really surprised us, until we did more research, and the logic became clear – so we built an extra step into our Not A Victim process.

---

18 Committee on Injury, Violence, and Poison Prevention, 'Role of the Pediatrician in Youth Violence Prevention', *Pediatrics*, 124/1 (2009), 393–402, https://doi.org/10.1542/peds.2009-0943

Part Two of this book will explain what you can do to ensure that your child enjoys the magical moments and does not suffer the misery moments. We will then take you through the Not A Victim process step by step. But before moving on, we'll end Part One with another case study, which illustrates many of the points we've been discussing.

Matthew Polly is the best-selling author of *American Shaolin, Tapped Out* and *Bruce Lee: A Life*. His writing has also appeared in publications such as *The Washington Post* and *Esquire*. He is a Princeton University graduate and Rhodes Scholar, and a fellow at Yale University. He grew up in Topeka, Kansas, spent two years studying kung fu at the Shaolin Temple in Henan, China, and now lives in New Haven, Connecticut.

BULLYING BREAKTHROUGH 3: MATTHEW

The bullying started at elementary school. I had the annoying habit of knowing the answers to the teachers' questions. That, of course, annoyed the other boys, so they took their frustrations out on me. When I didn't get the message, they would hold me down and hit me more. I never told my parents about it; I found it too shameful. Sometimes I would run away, hoping they didn't catch me. Sometimes I'd just take the hit and drop my head, employing the 'Gandhi strategy'. I had the belief that if I kept up passive resistance long enough, it would stop it. But it didn't.

Looking back, I know it would have ended if I'd fought back, but I was too afraid to fight. That continued to bother me later in life. The terror that paralyses you means you let yourself be a victim. What I learned in the long run was that bullies take advantage of weakness. They don't like strength and they don't like someone who fights back. They don't actually want a fight; they just want to hurt somebody easily. That was the mistake I made as a child.

I never stopped studying or doing well at school but growing up I never thought that being smart was a good thing; being smart was what got you hit. The biggest effect of being bullied was that by the time I was a teenager I just wanted to leave and get out of my home town. So I left and went to college at Princeton, which is full of smart kids. Suddenly, I had an entire group of people around me who were the same as me. That's where I started studying martial arts. I made friends, had girlfriends, felt normal – at least, I didn't feel different from everyone else. I wasn't bullied anymore.

The biggest insight I have gained on this subject is that when you stand up for yourself, other people respect you. I'm highly engaged in making my five-year-old son bully-proof. He takes Tae Kwon Do and I mildly tease and joke with him a lot, so he is comfortable with verbal roughhousing. Most of all, I encourage him not to back down when something bad happens. You want your child to be polite and mannerly, but you don't want them to be an easy target for bullies.

PART TWO
ENDING THE CYCLE OF BULLYING

If we do not learn through and from bullying, if we are not able to view bullying in the right context and challenge the situation, then the tragic reality is that bullying will recur throughout your child's life and into adulthood. Regardless of where you are right now in the journey, the age of your children, your level of understanding and involvement, or the date that you happen to be reading this, there are some things you can implement right now that can help you take the first, or further, steps toward helping your child break through bullying.

5
Getting In Training

We believe that a higher value should be placed on a child's character than on their grades or academic success. So much emphasis and pressure is put onto 'scoring' children, from an early age, on their academic ability, but there is little focus on applying a progressive structure to the development of their character. Yet there is striking evidence that from an early age, measurements of executive function and cognitive fitness are highly predictive of children's future achievement, even when controlling for IQ scores or socio-economic status.[19]

We passionately believe that developing your child's character should be the number one goal for all parents,

---

19 'Executive Function Skills for Student Success', Bill & Melinda Gates Foundation (BMGF, 2019) in association with Intentional Futures, p1.

teachers and the education system. A child's character is their moral compass and ultimately affects every decision they make, from the relationships and friendships they form to the goals they set, the vision they aspire to and the daily habits they follow. It's the most important aspect of a child's development and yet it's so often the missing ingredient in their education.

But what exactly is a child's 'character' and how can we 'develop' it? In 2017, we conducted a survey with over 2,000 parents of children in the Warrior Academy to identify what constituted character. The result was the 3Cs: conduct, confidence and concentration. A child will typically have high levels of one or two of the 3Cs, but rarely all three. By developing all of them to a high level a child achieves what we call a 'black belt character', which will set them up for a successful and happy adult life.

Your first task is to identify, in your child, which C needs bringing up to the level of the other two. We call this the child's 'breakthrough area'. It's the area you need to focus on first to achieve the quickest development in your child's character. You can discover your child's breakthrough area by visiting www.breakthrougharea.com.

Next, it's time for some mental training.

Michael Gervais says that there are only three things we can train: our craft, our body and our mind (which we will call our brain).[20] Society is focused principally on our craft and in different ways also on our bodies. Our mind is only just beginning to come to the surface.

This may be to do with how easy it is to measure progress in each of these three areas. Craft is easy to measure. You go to school, where you either pass or fail your exams, and there are things you can do to improve your 'score'. When you work for a company, your performance is tracked and measured, and you have annual conversations with your employer where you discuss ways you can improve.

Similarly, when it comes to the physical, we have so many ways of measuring our bodies. We have images of what is the 'norm'. However, some of these can be misleading. We might see a person who looks athletic and muscular but has a limp because there's something wrong with their balance or coordination. We are told that if we feel stiff, we must be getting 'old', but these two things don't necessarily go hand in hand.

Training the brain, on the other hand, presents certain challenges. We can't easily measure or observe the capacity of our brain because we can't easily look inside it. Even if we could, we wouldn't know what

---

20 Michael Gervais, 'As humans, we can only train three things' (25 September 2020), www.instagram.com/p/CFkf8jvsvWW, accessed 8 May 2021

to look for. If we can't measure something, the judgement as to whether we are improving it or not becomes subjective. Yet through science, it has become possible to monitor how our brains work and to measure how efficient our cognitive functions are – in other words, our mental fitness.

Mental fitness

Training the brain can be compared to taking supplements. People take supplements if their nutritional needs are not being met through their diet and lifestyle. It's the same with going to the gym when we aren't getting enough movement into our days. Training your child's brain can be viewed similarly. If there is a deficit, or you simply want to create more capacity, training is a way to do so. Once they have reached the required level, you simply need to maintain that level.

In our assessment app that we mentioned earlier, is a game that trains all five cognitive domains. You can't choose what game you play, that's determined by your cognitive fitness score. For example, if you score low on executive function, your game will give you more training on that, while still making sure you train the other four cognitive domains.

Of course, a game is not the only way to train your brain. There are many other ways of improving your mental fitness, things most people know about already, but either don't do or aren't consistent in:

- Getting proper sleep
- Moving every day
- Keeping yourself flexible
- Continuing to learn
- Eating well
- Drinking enough water
- Taking recharge breaks
- Continuing to adapt and make things challenging
- Allowing yourself full and active recovery
- Doing things with passion/love
- Having quality time for yourself
- Having quality time with others
- Using stress to your advantage, not staying under pressure for too long

Mental fitness encompasses the processes that enable you to focus, understand, and respond with speed and accuracy; to store and retrieve, and remember information; to plan, process, and solve problems; and to think of the consequences of your actions before undertaking them. Your personality, emotions and values are all linked to your mental fitness.

We want you and your family to be in peak mental fitness, so that you can break through bullying (and life's other obstacles). We want you to earn a black belt in resilience.

Black belt in resilience

The concept of a black belt in resilience is summed up in the acronym BBR, where the first B stands for **bounce back**, which is what you must be able to do when attacked. The force of a physical or mental attack doesn't dictate or predict its impact on you, but your (in)ability to recover from it – to move from set-back to comeback – does. As we have seen, stress isn't intrinsically harmful, but failure to recover from it is. Our Not A Victim process will teach you how to get back to your optimal state and how to do so quickly; you, in turn, can teach this to your child.

The second B stands for **bounce attack**, which is about responding to attacks, both physically and mentally. This will enable you to take on more stress without it affecting you, enabling you to face even greater challenges.

Finally, the R stands for **readiness and resilience**, which is about applying the principles and processes you have learned from common life challenges so that they affect you much less, or for less time, than before – or not at all. It's a state of calm readiness. Anxiously waiting for something to happen is not readiness, because this state is tiring and does not put you in the best position to deal with the situation when it arises. It's also about situational awareness, where you don't put yourself in situations that involve risk. When confronted, you know how to work your way through it, even in situations that are new to you.

The dark side vs the wake-up call

In the previous chapter we looked at three magical moments and three misery moments that your child can experience when going through bullying. One way of making sure your child benefits the magic moments and not the misery moments is through explaining what we call the dark side versus the wake-up call. The steps of the dark side lead to the misery moments, and those of the wake-up call to the magical moments.

DARK stands for: **D**isconnect, (mal)**A**dapt, **R**estrict, **K**amikaze.

If your child is being bullied, they may Disconnect from what is happening, because it's distressing, and it hurts. Their body has no option but to Adapt to this, but it is a mal adaptation: the body goes into flight mode and your child feels stressed, anxious and fearful. This might cause them to Restrict themselves – not only in terms of avoiding certain places but also not allowing themselves to grow, out of a desire for self-protection. Because they don't like feeling like fearful and restricted, they might start using substances or self-harming, which is kamikaze – the self-destruction stage.

CALL stands for: **Connect, Adapt, Live, Love.**

To avoid the dark side and, instead of a misery moment, experience a magical moment, your child must connect with what is happening to them. It might not be nice, but at least they will be able to see which way to go. Then they can adapt to the situation and continue growing. They will do this by taking small steps, each of which is challenging but not insurmountable. Through being curious instead of restricted, they can enhance their life, which in turn will enable them to love life. This is evidently what we want to achieve, so let's look at the wake-up call in more detail.

Connect: Now is D-Day

All memorable moments are created in the now, not when you are occupied with the past or present. This is why it is so important for your child to connect to what is happening to them, however unpleasant they might find it. We call the present moment 'D-Day' because we believe that there are no big or small moments. There is only now, the key moment, the moment for taking action: D-Day. You might not like what is happening, but it is happening, right now, and you need to connect with it. Be honest about what is happening to you and face up to how you are feeling.

The alternative is to do nothing, hoping the problem will go away by itself. Which it won't.

Adapt: + 4%

Once you are connected to what is happening, you can start to see how best to adapt to it. This comes through learning and planning. What many people get wrong is to go straight from idea to implementation, without first taking the time to learn and form a strategy. Or, they don't adapt at all and find themselves on the dark side.

Why +4%? We often underestimate what we are capable of. In chapter two, we talked about flow. One of the pathways to flow is to make what you want to do a little more difficult than what you are capable of. When a challenge is too small, you can lose interest in it; when it is too big, you can become anxious about it. We say that the ideal level to aim for is 4% more than you think you can achieve. The moment you think about giving up, or not daring to do or say something, you can always be 4% braver, push 4% more. If you do this daily, within just eighteen days, you will have increased your capability by 100%.

Live: Make way for magic

When you do what you've always done, things usually don't change, so there is no need for you to adapt. What makes you come alive is opening yourself up to new experiences and ideas. Even when you are doing something you have done before, it is important to be open. What is magical about the situation you are in? Or, if it's a negative situation, how can you create something magical out of it? We both went through bullying and from those experiences we have created this book, turning something that was painful and made us feel like nothing into something magical.

Love: Add a bit of love to all you do

If you are going to do something, add a bit of love to it. Add love to the activity you are doing, to the conversation you are having. Have the self-confidence to believe that you are good enough to be loved, to do things you love and to love others. Keep falling in love with yourself, your activities, your environment and the people around you.

Before moving on to the Not A Victim process itself, we would like to share another story that illustrates many of the themes we have been discussing in this chapter. Jason Graystone is an investor who has developed educational businesses that teach people how to achieve financial independence. During his last year of high school, he experienced bullying:

BULLYING BREAKTHROUGH 4 : JASON

It was mental bullying, never physical. I was badly threatened, which meant that I couldn't focus on my school work and exams. Most of my last year in high school I ate lunch in the toilet and left school before the bell rang. There were times when I didn't eat or sleep, and spent my Sundays sweating at the prospect of going to school the next day. My friends were no help, as they preferred to be part of 'the gang'.

My parents had regular meetings with the teachers and with other parents but, as the bullying wasn't physical, there was no evidence. That made it hard for the school to deal with and this lack of action made it hard for me, as I was branded with the image of being mad and/or paranoid.

I passed my exams but got poor grades. The experience was so horrendous that when I left school, I completely deleted it from my mind. Today, I cannot remember one teacher's name and hardly any of my schoolmates.

The bullying not only contributed to my poor marks, it also had an impact on my confidence and on my subsequent employment. Although the period of bullying was limited, it held me back for a long time afterwards.

Leaving school was a moment of transformation. I was overweight and unhealthy, so I decided to start running and getting fit. I lost weight and started feeling good. I thought: Those bullies can't touch me now. That gave me more confidence and, over the next couple of years, I trained hard, as well as reading a lot and teaching myself new things. I felt empowered. It was quite a revelation, I realised that bullies are only there if your mind allows them to be.

I believe that in every area we're not empowered in, we get pushed around. We need to empower ourselves, because once we do that, the bullies disappear; they simply dissolve.

Looking back, I can see that I should have stood up against my bullies, told them that I wasn't scared and had nothing to be ashamed about. But I was scared, and the way I acted made me look guilty. I believe that everything that happens to us can help us in some way. I teach my kids: you can be, do, have whatever you want. It's your mindset that decides how you perceive everything that happens to you. No matter what happens to you, there is a positive and a negative side to it. There is always a benefit and a drawback to every situation.

If someone tells you you're fat, or hurts you in another way, look at it as a positive and say, 'Yes, I'm going to work on that' and thank them for it. If you are physically bullied, empower yourself by working on your health and fitness. Do sports, try martial arts. If you feel empowered, you give off an aura that says, 'Don't come near me.'

When my son started high school, there were a couple of kids he said he hated. I sat down with him and asked, 'What do you admire about those kids?' And he said, 'Nothing.' I said, 'No, there are just as many things that you admire about them as you hate about them, trust me.' We talked for half an hour and by the end of it he was saying, 'Oh yeah, he's good at basketball... He's got a long-term girlfriend... He's really loyal... He's quite funny...' I could see a weight come off his shoulders.

It made him think differently about that situation, and about other situations. Whenever anything negative happens, or you're under pressure, try to think about the positives. Who is looking out for you, who is supporting you? Whenever there's a challenge, there's support somewhere.

Seeing both the positives and the negatives helps you to make balanced decisions. In my work, I see people make decisions based only on greed. It's not just that they are naive about money, they also have unrealistic fantasies. As soon as they're aware of this, they feel empowered and don't make the same mistakes again.

6

The Not A Victim Process: Part One

As we have seen, a child that is not mentored correctly through bullying will be bullied for far longer than necessary, because the majority of children who experience bullying have not yet developed the cognitive fitness or emotional intelligence to understand why bullying occurs and how to deal with it.

Over the years, we have developed a system to help mentor students through bullying. Not A Victim is a step-by-step process for mentoring your child and yourself through the transition of bullying. In this and the following chapter, we will explain how it works.

The 6Ps

The emphasis of the first phase of our process focuses on the child: directly enabling the child, giving them the tools and understanding they need, empowering them to navigate this transition and move positively through it. The emphasis of the second phase focuses on the parents, who can feel overwhelmed and hopeless as they send their child to school each day unable to help them, unable to look after them and control the outcome of the day, knowing that their child must go through this and grow from the experience so that it does not repeat itself.

Step One: Perception

The word 'bully' comes from the sixteenth century Dutch word *boele*, meaning 'lover'. Originally, it was a term of endearment. Later, it became a familiar form of address for a male friend, meaning something like 'good fellow'. Later still, it was used to describe a daredevil. Only relatively recently did it acquire its modern meaning. As we can see, perceptions of what a 'bully' is have changed over the centuries – and the first step in our process is to change your and your child's perceptions of bullying.

We have seen that bullying appears to be a learned behaviour and that there is a real danger of the child who has been bullied continuing the cycle. There are some fantastic initiatives in schools to help educate and raise awareness of the subject, but sadly these often lack follow-through and there is little training for staff in this area.

We have also seen that, in almost all cases, bullies bully because they are missing something, and it makes them feel better. Bullying shows a weakness of character, not strength. Changing the perception of the bully from a threat to someone we should feel sorry for reduces the fear of being bullied and prevents us from reacting with aggression or distress. If we respond in this way, a bully has gained the reaction they needed to reinforce their position as the dominant person in the social setting, and the bully–victim relationship is reinforced.

So many young people don't report bullying because they blame themselves. Reframing bullying will help your child open up about their experiences and encourage them to participate in the next 5Ps. This first step is so powerful that many of the young people we have worked with find they overcome bullying within a week after changing their perception.

Nevertheless, we often find resistance from parents at this first step in the process. When they discover that their child has been bullied, they are emotionally hurt, they feel guilty: 'Why did this happen? How could I have done things differently to prevent it? Why wasn't I there for my child?' In many cases, parents feel more pain and heartache than their child, as children have a natural ability to forgive. Your child wants to forgive their bully and live a life without conflict, but often it's the parents who prevent them from doing so and subconsciously build barriers around their child, preventing them from reframing and changing the context of bullying: 'How can I possibly tell my child to forgive their bully after they have been hurting them for so long?'

Our response is to ask parents: 'What if you *don't* teach them to forgive the bully?' By not forgiving them, they will hold onto these feelings of anger, frustration and emotional distress for years. We ask parents to 'self-ishly forgive' the bully, because they are not doing it for the bully, but for their child.

You should explain to your child that bullying happens for a multitude of reasons. Break down bullying for them, as we did in chapter three. In the process, you will teach your child valuable life lessons and develop their emotional intelligence. It's a difficult process for both parent and child, but a rewarding journey to go on together.

Here is an exercise you can do with your child.

STORY EXERCISE

We find the best way to pass knowledge onto a child is to tell a story, followed by a series of questions to highlight the main points. You can tailor the story to the age or maturity of your child.

Introduce the main character as a kind, fun friend. Then talk in detail about a difficult time this character is going through, including age-specific challenges or incidences that your child will relate to. These can include:

- Being bullied at school
- Not doing well in class/at their sports club
- Losing a relative/grandparent
- Going through parental separation

Explain how, through these events, your character felt incredibly upset and had nowhere to turn. They began to react to people around them in a negative way, to bully others. The context here is that the character is not bad; the flow of negative energy is what has caused them to pick on other people and become a bully.

Your questions should lead your child to an understanding of why the bullying occurred and ultimately to a reframing of their opinion of the bully. Your questions can follow this format:

- Do you remember the start of our story?
    - Do you think (character) was a nice person?
- Do you think what happened to them was sad?
    - How would you feel if that happened to you?
- How do you think (character) felt when those bad things happened to them?
    - Do you think they were angry, sad, frustrated, scared?
- Do you think that if (character) hadn't had those horrible things happen to them, they wouldn't be bullying other people?
    - Do you think that people who bully do it because they are sad, scared, or angry about something bad that has happened to them?

- Can you see that (character) is not a bad person, but has just had bad things happen to them?
    - Should we be scared of (character) or should we feel sorry for them?
- Imagine that your friend is going through what (character) is going through. How do you think you could help them?
- If you experienced this yourself, how would you like to be supported to overcome it?

When you have gone through this process, ask your child some more general questions, such as:

- What traits do you think the bully has that are good?
- What traits does the bully have that you admire?
- Do you have those traits too?
- Would you like to have those traits?

The answers to these questions may surprise you both.

One final point on perception is that it is not just your child's perception of the bully that is important, but also their perception of themselves. The more your child likes themselves and trusts in their own abilities, the less chance they have of becoming a victim. We often think we like ourselves more than other people, and yet we care more about their opinions than our own. But these opinions constantly change with passing trends, so when your child accepts an outside opinion over their own, they too must constantly change, which is hard to keep up with.

Step Two: Presentation

Body language is such an important part of communication, so we place huge emphasis on it in our work. A bully is far less likely to target someone who appears strong or confident, so we teach our students that the way they walk, talk, hold themselves, maintain eye contact, and even shake hands, is vital.

When you are happy, you smile; and when you smile, you feel happy – a principle first noted by William James.[21] Our behaviours, or what our body is physically doing, can trigger emotions – in ourselves and in people around us. While the concept is simple, the effect is profound. Instilling the knowledge that by changing your behaviour you will influence your emotional state is more effective than trying to deal with the challenges on a psychological level and is a practical way to help your child through bullying.

In our work, we encourage parents to ask their child to paint a picture of a confident individual – the opposite of a bully – and then to imagine that they are that individual. The effect can be amazing. After a period of time practising being confident, confidence becomes a natural part of the child's personality. With this new-found confidence, they no longer appear an easy target.

---

21   W James, *The Gospel of Relaxation* (Scribner's, 1899)

Here is a practical exercise you can do with your child to improve their body language and confidence:

BODY LANGUAGE EXERCISE

Be aware of your child's body language at home, at school (if possible), in their sports club, in public in terms of the traits listed. Does your child:

1. Avoid eye contact? ☐
2. Cross their arms in a social situation? ☐
3. Keep their hands in their pockets? ☐
4. Rarely smile or laugh? ☐
5. Avoid being in the centre of the room? ☐
6. Hunch their shoulders? ☐
7. Slouch? ☐
8. Touch their face? ☐
9. Keep their chin and head down? ☐
10. Talk quickly? ☐
11. Fidget a lot? ☐
12. Have fast or shallow breathing (through the mouth)? ☐

Talk through each point with your child and come up with a list of five areas you'd like to work on. Just by improving these five, you will see a radical improvement in their non-verbal communication. They will appear more confident and, as they start to see the difference in how people respond to them, they will feel more confident. This change typically occurs within ten days, with consistent practice.

Turning the twelve body language traits from the previous exercise on their head, we can see why overcoming them increases confidence.

Maintain eye contact

Good eye contact is a clear sign of confidence. A trait typical of someone going through bullying is to avoid eye contact and look down, which gives a submissive appearance and reinforces the impression of being a victim. Learning to hold eye contact can be empowering for a child. Teach your child, when they are talking to someone, to look at a point between their eyes. It's important, of course, not to hold eye contact for too long, which can be seen as intimidating.

Also teach your child to nod when they are listening. This will help them build rapport with the person they are communicating with, which is an important way to feel comfortable, happy and confident in their environment. Mirroring is a more advanced version of this and can be taught to older teens (sixteen and older).

Adopt an open posture

Folded arms and hands in pockets are an indicator of low confidence, nervousness, or anxiety in a social situation, a classic defensive posture. In contrast, speaking with our arms when we are explaining something or making a point, or responding with a gesture, is a sign of confidence.

Make positive facial expressions

A smile or a laugh goes a long way. A frown or a negative facial expression is a sign of insecurity and discomfort. We teach our students to smile whenever they enter a room. In doing so, they put themselves in a confident state by framing the environment to match how they want to feel. This gives them more control of their emotions and feelings than they realise.

Don't be afraid to take up space

A child going through bullying will often look for opportunities to avoid attention. This tendency is all too clear to those who are doing the bullying. By moving into the centre of a room, your child will appear more confident. Keeping their hands out of their pockets and gesturing with their hands, as discussed, helps them to take up more space and shows that they are in control of their environment, that they are confident in and happy with their surroundings.

Relax your shoulders

Rounded or hunched shoulders (often due to hands in pockets) signal a desire to hide, to become smaller and less of a target. More importantly, it makes us feel smaller and less confident. A relaxed posture shows that we are comfortable and happy in our environment, that we are not a victim.

Stand upright

This is a big one. Much like relaxing our shoulders, maintaining an upright posture and opening up our chest is vital to coming across as confident. It also impacts the way we sound and how our voice projects. It's incredible how quickly correcting this negative trait transforms our appearance. We need constant reminders for this to become a habit. A tip is to teach your child to imagine they are suspended from the ceiling by an invisible thread.

Don't touch your face or bite your nails

We often try to hide our face with our hands if we are nervous, anxious or uneasy. Many nervous children cover their mouths as they speak. Remind your child that their hands are needed for gesturing, as discussed. Nail-biting is a similar manifestation of nervousness or anxiety. If your child habitually bites their nails, you could try using a product with an unpleasant taste, that is applied to their nails.

Keep your head up

A lowered head is a clear indication of nervousness. It's another way of 'hiding', of making ourselves small. Teaching your child to raise their head, especially when they are talking, is really important.

Slow down

We often talk faster when we are nervous. We want the situation to pass quickly because we are uncomfortable with it. Slowing down our speech (and our movements) makes us look and feel more in control of and comfortable in our environment.

Stop fidgeting

Fidgeting is a classic symptom of nervousness and anxiety. A cool, calm and collected individual who is happy in their environment and not nervous or anxious doesn't fidget.

Give a firm handshake

A handshake is one of the first things we do as adults when we meet someone new. It may not be so important for children and teenagers but it's a habit worth developing from a young age. A firm, slightly prolonged handshake affirms that we are happy, confident and in control.

Breathe through the nose calmly and slowly

When we are nervous or anxious, our rate of breathing increases and the depth of our breathing reduces. We often breathe through our mouths and our breathing can be audible. Your child can change all other aspects of their body language, but if they don't work on their breathing, their confidence will be limited. Breathing slowly and deeply is one of the quickest ways to get into the optimal state. Remind your child to breathe through their nose, right down into their abdomen, with a particular focus on slow exhalation.

Vocal cues

It can be helpful to use vocal cues to encourage the desired body language. As you are building habits, you need to be consistent in your approach. Constantly explaining why this or that is important will only put your child off, whereas a quick word will remind them instantly. Once the habit is developed, they will find this word jumping into their mind whenever they touch their face or bow their head. Here are some vocal cues you can use, depending on your child's needs:

- Eyes – when they avoid eye contact
- Head / chin – when they drop their chin or look down
- Hands – when they cover their face or bite their nails
- Calm – when they speak too quickly or fidget
- Pockets – when they put their hands in their pockets

- Space – when they head for a corner of the room
- Smile – when they enter a room
- Chest – when they slump or slouch
- Breathe – when their breathing becomes quick or shallow

Step Three: Preparation

Whenever we do anything in a high-stress environment or are overwhelmed emotionally, we are unable to think or react clearly and our judgement tends to be affected. Of the three Fs, we tend to choose flight or freeze. Typically, in a bullying situation, these responses only reinforce the bully–victim relationship and ensure that it continues.

In our work, in almost every case where a child has learned to make the transition through bullying, there is a clear – and often memorable – moment of decision in which the child stands up to their bully. However, it is not necessary for your child to have already experienced bullying to learn how to respond to it. It is a matter of preparation, and you can practise responding to bullying with your child at home.

Just as a martial artist prepares to block a strike by drilling the same technique 100 times a day for months on end, or a lecturer might practise a speech dozens of times before stepping on stage, you can rehearse the necessary response until it becomes second nature. Like a muscle memory, it will be your child's natural reaction if and when the situation arises.

The perfect response to a bully or a bullying situation should do five things:

1. Protect us from harm

2. Stop the bullying in its tracks

3. Deconstruct the bully–victim relationship

4. Remind us that the bully has no power over us

5. Not escalate the situation into a physical confrontation

Here is an exercise that will help you and your child achieve all five of these things:

RESPONSE EXERCISE

Work with your child to brainstorm quick and easy-to-remember come-backs that will make them appear confident when they are being bullied. Simple, non-aggressive phrases work best. Use words that come naturally to your child, that they will feel confident saying. Refine the list until you have ten to twenty responses. To get you started, here are a few examples that we have found work well:

- Go away
- Stop
- Who cares?
- Whatever
- Sure
- Yeah, right
- You're so funny!

As you will see, some of these responses use sarcasm. This can be a useful tactic, but approach it with caution and be sure that your child understands it. (It has been shown that children don't begin to understand sarcasm until they are around six years old.)[22]

If your child has a full grasp of sarcasm and is able to use it confidently, a great way of de-escalating bullying is to agree with the bully. For example, if your child is called 'dumb' or 'stupid' by the bully, they might respond with, 'Yes, I sometimes do dumb stuff.' With the possible sarcastic addition of, 'Not everyone can be smart like you!' or 'How did you become so smart?'

Like all the exercises in this chapter, planning these responses is a method that needs practice, which is the subject of the next step.

---

22   University of Manitoba, 'Getting Sarcastic With Kids', *Science Daily* (9 August 2007), www.sciencedaily.com/releases/2007/08/070803141811.htm, accessed 8 May 2021

7

The Not A Victim Process: Part Two

In this chapter we'll continue looking at the 6Ps of the Not A Victim process, moving on to the fourth P: Practice.

Step Four: Practice

The last step was about the importance of preparation. It's highly unlikely that you will be there to help your child when they are being bullied, so a big part of your role in mentoring them to overcome bullying lies in the preparation. But it's equally important for your child to practise the behaviours and responses you've prepared so that they can respond quickly and confidently if a bullying situation arises.

We have found that the most effective tool for practising for the difficult situation of bullying is role playing.

ROLE PLAY EXERCISE

In this exercise, explain to your child that you would like them to be the bully and you will be the person who is bullied. If they have already been bullied, watching what they do and say here will give you some insight into what they have been through. React using the words and phrases you have prepared together. Watch how your child responds: this is how they expect their bully to respond. They are mirroring the learned behaviour of bullying they have witnessed.

You can now adjust your responses based on this new knowledge. After you have found the perfect response, it's time to switch roles. Be careful here and start off lighthearted, then up the intensity slightly. Again, it's important this is tailored to the age and emotional stability of your child. If you push too hard in your role as the bully, you can build barriers instead of breaking them down. Add new words, sentences and actions – such as standing over them – gradually. Remember that the ideal way to progress is using the 4% principle, where the challenge is just beyond your child's current skillset and state.

The idea is to go over the same routine several times until your child can confidently and effectively respond without thinking. You will watch them grow in confidence quickly through this activity, and often it's quite good fun.

Try to make role playing a daily habit – when your child comes home from school, for example. You will find that, once you have the communication lines open, you will see big improvements quickly. Practice makes perfect – and confidence.

This exercise does six interesting and powerful things:

It empowers: Role playing with your child will empower them. They will feel better equipped and more confident about dealing with the situation. If you do it enough, you will notice a change in them: their anxiety will be replaced by a feeling of empowerment.

It gives you deeper insight: If you take on the role of the child being bullied and your child takes on the role of the bully, you will both get a much deeper insight into what is happening in their bullying situation.

It teaches your child how not to respond: A typical response to bullying is to strike back, but this can land your child in more trouble. If your child gets bullied and responds aggressively, they might be seen as the bully. Developing a strong state of mind and social skills to overcome the bullying is far more effective and is a more sustainable, healthy response to confrontation.

It gives them confidence: At first, your child may be unsure of the effectiveness of the words and phrases they have chosen to use in response to bullying. The role play gives them an opportunity to practise, which will give them the confidence to use these words in a real situation.

It increases their cognitive fitness: Through role play you are building pathways for handling novel and difficult situations, which will increase your child's overall cognitive fitness and resilience. This is the foundation of flow and the door to the three magical moments.

It improves communication and trust: Through role play you will also build a better, more open and honest relationship with your child. Your communication will rapidly improve and you will be spending more quality time together. By teaching them not to be afraid of bullying and regard confrontation in social situations as normal and something they can transition through without a strong emotional reaction, they will be prepared. They will think, 'My parents told me this would happen. Now I know exactly what to do.'

By taking these steps *before* your child is bullied, you will prevent them from feeling guilty and so make them more likely to confide in you straightaway if it does occur.

Step Five: Produce

This is an important step. One of the most upsetting situations you can find yourself in, as a parent, is when your child finally has the courage to talk about the bullying they have been experiencing for days, weeks or months. One day, they come home in tears and tell you all about it. It's upsetting for everyone and you feel an overwhelming urge to protect your child. You speak directly to the school and even the parents of the bullies, but what usually then happens is that the parents of the bullies (and sometimes even the school) deny everything: 'My child/X would never do that.' Naturally, a parent won't want to believe that their child is a bully. This is common. In fact, some parents react so defensively that the complaint is flipped and your child is accused of being the bully; we have seen and heard this countless times. Unfortunately, it's often the bully's word against your child's – and if there is more than one bully, your child will be outnumbered.

How can you overcome this? Rather than approaching the situation emotionally, you need to approach it logically and systematically. Teach your child the 5Ws of reporting bullying:

- Who

- What

- When

- Where

- Witnesses

It's essential to keep a written log of incidents, so give your child a notebook for this purpose. Then, if a situation arises where it is your child's word against the bullies', you can produce a dated list of occurrences with the names of witnesses who can corroborate the details. This will give huge credibility to your case.

This is also an exercise that can be practised in the safety of your home.

LOG EXERCISE

Buy your child a notebook and ask them to write up an imagined (or real) report of incidents of bullying they have experienced, ticking off all of the 5Ws. After a little practice, this will become an automatic part of your child's response to bullying.

This exercise can also be linked with role playing. For each occurrence listed, you can ask your child, 'What is the best way to respond to this situation?' and then practise their responses.

Step Six: Persevere

We spoke earlier in the book about the immense importance of a solid, supportive and stable community outside of your child's school environment (where bullying most frequently occurs) in helping, guiding and mentoring them through the experience of bullying. There are four main benefits of such a community:

Provides emotional support: A positive community helps a young person deal with failure or defeat by teaching them to put the ups and downs of life into perspective and ensuring that they learn the value of perseverance. We've seen this have the biggest impact on young people dealing with the loss of a loved one, separation of parents or moving schools – the three transitions – reducing the harmful effects of these highly stressful situations.

A positive community also promotes mutual support and the importance of empathy. This teaching will remain with them, influencing how they raise their own children. We learn so much from our peers, and empathy is a social skill that increases our emotional intelligence and improves our character.

What's more, in a positive community a young person develops relationships with other members and enjoys spending time in the community. This will make them happier. By promoting healthy competition, for instance in a sports club, members of a supportive community can build each other up.

Promotes health and fitness: If the positive community is sports or activity-related, young people develop a physical routine that promotes a healthy lifestyle. This can prevent obesity, stave off health problems and reduce the chances of anxiety and depression. A community of this kind typically understands the importance of and encourages healthy eating. This can stay with a young person for life, helping to avoid nutritional problems. In this way, such a community promotes a healthy lifestyle, which will ensure that the young person enjoys being active and thinks of healthy activity as a part of normal daily life.

Provides inspiration: By providing inspiration, a positive community will increase a young person's aspirations, encouraging them to strive to be the best they can be, changing how they see themselves and what they aspire to become. It also helps to develop their mindset and, more immediately, their confidence and self-worth.

A positive community gives a young person perspective on life, encouraging them to see the 'big picture' and giving a deeper meaning to life's challenges and successes. This perspective will inspire the young person to seek out bigger problems to solve so they can have a greater impact and become a leader in their community.

Encourages challenge and adventure: A positive community will build independence in a young person as they seek out challenges and make their own important decisions. This is a skill that will dramatically increase their ability to deal with peer pressure, which will be less likely to influence them in a negative way as they become accustomed to making and feeling confident in their own decisions.

This will increase the young person's resilience in stressful situations, give them the ability to lead and inspire others and empower them in their own lives. It will improve resourcefulness. When tackling challenges in the community, a young person has to think on their feet, and they can go on to apply this process to dealing with other challenges that life throws at them. As the American author, coach and philanthropist Tony Robbins said, 'It's not the lack of resources, it's your lack of resourcefulness that stops you.'[23]

Through the process of setting and achieving goals, a positive community can greatly increase a young person's confidence and self-esteem. It can enrich the young person's life by giving them more opportunities to explore, encouraging them to learn more about the world they live in.

To discover whether or not your child is part of a positive community, you can use the following exercise. If you would like to do this exercise online, go to www. notavictim.co.uk and follow the link to the Community Analyser tool.

COMMUNITY ANALYSIS EXERCISE

Consider the four principal communities that are present in your child's life and list the different groups within each community:

23   T Robbins (@TonyRobbins) 'It's not the lack of…' (22 January 2018) https://twitter.com/tonyrobbins/status/955455778512605184?lang=en, accessed 24 March 2021

- **School:** Friends, classes
- **Online:** Instagram and other social media
- **Home:** Siblings, other family, neighbours
- **Clubs:** After-school and extracurricular clubs and societies

Thinking about all the groups within those communities, rate each community in relation to the following ten statements. For each 'Yes', score 1 point. For each 'No', score 0 points.

1. My child speaks highly of others in this community.
2. This community gives my child interesting, creative ideas that they share with me.
3. This community enjoys physical activity together.
4. This community has always been a positive influence.
5. I'm not aware if my child has ever been bullied in this community.
6. After spending time with this community, my child feels inspired to achieve.
7. My child looks up to other members of this community and talks about them regularly.
8. My child is encouraged to help out at this community and to lead others.
9. This community always encourages my child to achieve more.
10. My child is regularly rewarded for their success in this community.

Add up the scores for each community and multiply the total by ten. This will give you a percentage that indicates the extent to which that community is a positive and supportive one. A powerful, supportive and positive community will score between 70% and 100%. A less valuable community will score between 50% and 70% and we recommend limiting the amount of time your child spends in this community, or removing them from it entirely.

A community with a score of under 50% is likely to be doing your child harm, so you should remove them from it quickly. If this is your child's 'home' community, you will need to establish which particular elements are potentially damaging, eg a babysitter, neighbour or friend.

The score you have given each community is subjective and your analysis can only be a rough guide, but it can be helpful to compare your child's communities and the value they contribute.

To summarise, a vital step to helping your child overcome bullying, now and in the future, is to ensure that they are part of strong, supportive communities and to remove them from any community that is likely to do them harm. Without a strong community, they can feel unworthy, isolated and lost.

If your child is being bullied, find a community outside the one they are being bullied within that will support them and fill them with confidence. Martial arts is just one example of such a community, which we have found helpful in overcoming bullying thanks to its focus on building confidence, developing a strong mind, handling confrontation and keeping calm in stressful situations.

Overview of the 6Ps

At this stage, you should have worked through each of the 6Ps and completed all of the exercises. Let's summarise where you and your child should be at now:

Step One: Perception – a new understanding

Both you and your child should now understand why bullying occurs, have put it into the right context and probably have quite a different viewpoint from the one you started out with. The feelings you have towards the bully may have switched from fear to pity; you may feel sorry for the bully, and so their power will have diminished or disappeared entirely. After completing this step, it is far less likely that your child will become a bully themselves, breaking the cycle of bullying.

Step Two: Presentation – better body language

In this step, your child will have learned the importance of non-verbal communication. After lots of practice and repetition using the vocal cues you developed, they will appear more confident when they walk into a room. Gradually, your child will begin to feel the way they look and you will start to see a big difference in their confidence and self-image, as well as in the image others have of them.

Step Three: Preparation – ready to respond

You and your child will have brainstormed the perfect responses to typical bullying situations, choosing comeback words or phrases for them to use in the moment without having to think, making them less likely to hesitate, stutter or sound unsure of themselves. Their response will be to 'fight' – not in the physical sense, but socially. As highlighted earlier, fighting back socially means standing up for yourself verbally, refusing to be submissive in a bullying situation and doing your best to prevent escalation to physical confrontation and re-occurrence in the future. The emphasis is shifted so the reaction of the 'target' steps away from being submissive and being seen as the reaction of a victim. They will not flee, freeze or be frightened.

Step Four: Practice – part of a team

Your child will have practised how to behave in every possible situation and be comfortable with how they will react. At the same time, you will have gained valuable insight into what they are going through. The exercises you have done will have empowered your child and opened up lines of communication between you. A huge part of mentoring your child through bullying is bringing you closer so that you feel like a team fighting this together.

Step Five: Produce – confidence through evidence

Your child will have an incident log (or know how to make one), which will be a valuable resource to provide evidence of the bullying they are experiencing if it's needed. This should give you the confidence to approach the school and/or other parents. Making a log is also a form of therapy, as your child may find it hard to speak about what they are going through and could be more comfortable writing about it.

Step Six: Persevere – supportive communities

Your community analysis will have given you a new perspective on the communities your child is currently part of. You may discover they are part of a negative community at home, in school or online, giving you the time and tools to quickly make a change before bullying occurs. You can also look for a community that will support them through their big three transitions and could help mentor them through bullying if it occurs.

The Not A Victim process, which has been developed over years of working with bullied children and their parents, is fundamental to ensuring that your child emerges from bullying stronger, more confident and with bucket-loads of courage. We know that, if your child is suffering from bullying, you will find value in the 6Ps.

PART THREE
A BLACK BELT IN RESILIENCE

As parents, we want our child to thrive and succeed. We want to give them the tools that will enable them to do so. If you think about your childhood, you will realise that you now live in a different world. The same will be true for your child: the world they become adults in will be quite different from the world they are growing up in. In the new information age, your child needs ever greater mental capacity, mental fitness and mental strength. They need a black belt in resilience.

8
Inspire And Heal

Once you have dealt with the immediate issue and impact of bullying, you can begin to think about how to ensure they can grow from the experience. According to Jonathan Haidt, 'Recent literature is beginning to address the notion that stress and trauma can actually be good for people,'[24] which suggests that some positives can be found in the experience of bullying.

We have looked at the practical steps you can take to help your child overcome bullying, but there is something more intangible you can do to make this transition not only smooth but also positive and life-enhancing: inspire.

---

24 J Haidt, *The Happiness Hypothesis; Putting Ancient Wisdom to the Test of Modern Science* (Random House, 2006)

Inspire your child through language

One of the most powerful tools you have as a parent is the language you use with your child, which literally paints a picture of the character they will grow into. When you describe your child, you create an image of them that they will model themselves on. Give them a role and they will grow into it.

One of the saddest things about bullying is that, after a while, we come to believe the words of the bully. The bully repeatedly paints a picture of a 'victim character' for us. The cumulative effect of that negative talk about us is huge. If we believe their negative words, we can give ourselves years of negative self-coaching.

We parents can also fall into this negativity trap. We have had countless parents tell us, in front of their child, the problems they wish to correct, from 'My son/daughter is fat, they need to lose weight' to, 'My child is nervous', 'My child is badly behaved', even 'They're a wimp.' This approach creates a self-fulfilling prophecy, as the child adopts the same negative self-talk and develops a host of insecurities. Not only can it slow the progress you make in overcoming bullying, it can lead to the worst possible outcomes: that your child never loses the victim mentality, or becomes a bully themselves.

It's easy for us to use positive language when our child is well behaved or comes home from school inspired, but we need to ensure that we use the same language regardless of our child's state.

Parental resilience

We've heard devastating stories from parents, of children being severely physically bullied, or finding notes in their child's school bag from classmates telling them they should kill themselves. Such experiences cause parents acute stress, which can lead to burn-out, sickness and other physical and emotional damage. Breaking through bullying is not just about helping our child to become resilient, we also need to develop this resilience ourselves.

To be resilient and be able to bounce back, we need vitality. Vitality is our ability to use our internal resources to do what we want and need to do – and then some, to have extra energy to take on the unplanned and the unpleasant.

To maintain our vitality, we need to do two things:

1. Keep our bodies and minds in peak condition
2. Escape the struggle/frustration zone as quickly as possible

Let's look at each of these challenges in turn.

Maintaining peak condition

There are eight primary areas we must manage to keep our bodies and minds in peak condition:

- Moving
- Breathing
- Eating
- Drinking
- Sleeping
- Charging
- Thinking
- Self-monitoring

In each case, there is a minimum and an optimal 'dose', the former being the minimum amount that you need to perform well. To ensure that you have at least this dose, there are several actions you can take in each of these areas.

Moving

Since most of us these days have a sedentary lifestyle, it's vital to keep moving and stay flexible. Otherwise, our minds and bodies can become stiff and lethargic. Make sure you move for thirty consecutive minutes every day. If you have a sedentary job, get up and move around every thirty minutes – and don't sit with your legs crossed.

Breathing

Most people have shallow, chest-focused breathing, often through the mouth. This can cause tension in your core and neck as well as create a state of excessive arousal, where a more relaxed state is preferable. To address this, note how many breaths you take in one minute when you are in a normal, relaxed state. The ideal is six to twelve. If your number is more than this, focus on breathing slowly and more deeply. Breathe through your nose and use your abdomen to force the air in and out of your lungs. When exercising, try to breathe through your nose; eventually, you will be able to do this instead of breathing through your mouth.

Try the CO_2 test and see if you need to increase your CO_2 tolerance through breathing work. Then, whenever you feel wrongly charged, do a set of box breathing. These exercises are described below:

BREATHING EXERCISES

CO2 test

Sit or stand comfortably. Breathe through your nose three times, normally. Then, breathe in as much as you can. As you begin to exhale through your nose, start your timer. Exhale as slowly as you can, for as long as possible. Stop the timer when you have no more air to exhale, or when you swallow or hold your breath. The number of seconds on the timer is your score. A score below twenty means there is a lot of room for improvement. Do your best to work up your score above forty or higher.

Breathing more effectively
Breathe through your nose throughout the day and night and try to reduce the number of breaths you take per minute, try to get this down to ten.

Box breathing
Box breathing is rhythmic breathing and consists of four stages of equal length: inhale, inhale hold, exhale and exhale hold. Both inhaling and exhaling should be through the nose. It's called box breathing because it's like going around a square where all the sides are the same length; for example: inhale for two seconds, hold for two seconds, exhale for two seconds, hold for two seconds. Choose the number of seconds according to the state you want to be in. If you want to increase your breathing capacity, choose a higher number that is challenging but doable; if you want to get into a more relaxed state, pick a number that feels comfortable.

Eating

We all know the importance of a good diet, but how and when we eat are just as important as what we eat. Some good rules of thumb are to:

- Put your fork, spoon or knife down after you have taken a bite

- Chew properly before swallowing

- Eat until you're 80% full

- Not eat within three hours of going to bed

Drinking

When we are dehydrated, both our physical and mental functions are impaired. You can calculate how much you should be drinking each day based on your size,[25] and should make sure you get that amount. A good practice is to drink a glass of water first thing in the morning.

Sleeping

Sleep, too, is vital to our wellbeing and there are several things you can do to make sure you are getting enough, and good quality, sleep. We recommend that you:

- Have a sleep routine, where you go to bed and wake up at the same time each day.

- When on holiday, don't set an alarm to give yourself a better indication of the amount of sleep you naturally need to recover. Go to bed when you feel tired and see when you wake up. Do this for a few days to gauge your optimum amount of sleep and you can then adapt your sleep routine accordingly.

---

25 GIGAcalculator, 'Daily Water Intake Calculator', www. gigacalculator.com/calculators/water-intake-calculator.php

- Try to get some daylight within an hour of waking up (ideally around sunrise) and get as much sunlight as possible throughout the day, making sure you see the sunset every day.

- Do your best to avoid bright light between 11pm and 4am because this can damage your biological clock and make it more difficult for you to sleep or reduce your sleep quality.

Charging

If we do all the things listed but don't stop all day, we will run out of fuel. We need to charge ourselves throughout the day. If you are tense or stressed, you will need to discharge rather than recharge. You should take regular charging breaks throughout the day: go for a walk or a drive, have a shower or do some breathing exercises. After your break, check that you feel recharged/discharged; if you don't, try something different.

Thinking

It's important to regularly take time to think. This may be during your charging breaks or at a different time. Journaling is a great way of managing your thoughts by putting them on paper, so try keeping a journal in which you write down three things you are grateful for each day. Just before you go to bed, write down a question you would like an answer to, or a problem you want to solve. Be as specific as possible. The moment you wake up, write any solutions that have occurred to you. It's amazing how often your subconscious finds the answer.

Self-monitoring

As we mentioned earlier, we need to develop our skills in reading and regulating our internal state. If you are tense or stressed when you eat or exercise, the benefits will not be as great as when you feel alert or relaxed. If you are feeling agitated when you talk to your child, it will be more difficult to have a positive, productive conversation.

To address this, you should constantly be mindful of the state you are in. The simplest and most effective way of regulating your state is through breathing. If you are feeling stressed, breathe more slowly, with an emphasis on exhaling. Try to breathe through your nose rather than through your mouth. If you are lacking in energy, breathe more rapidly, but still through your nose.

Getting out of the struggle/frustration zone

When we are struggling with something, we tend to get lost in it and it ends up consuming more energy than necessary. If it's something we have been through before, we know we can handle it, but if we encounter a new obstacle or challenge, we can lack the knowledge and confidence to deal with it quickly and effectively.

First, we must tell ourselves that we *can* figure it out. We must believe that we can do difficult things and remind ourselves of past experiences that back this up. Then we must focus on what we can control. When our child is being bullied, we can feel helpless, as if there is nothing we can do about it. This is not the case; there are many things we can do.

When we are in a struggle, it is hard to think clearly. A great way to get out of this is to be curious, asking questions like 'What's good about this situation?' 'What can I learn from this?' We often see parents focusing on the content instead of the context. The content is that their child is being bullied at school. The context is the transition they are going through: bullying is part of a bigger picture. Recognising this can help you to refocus your attention on the action you can take. As we have said before, you want to maintain an environment where your child can come to you with any problem at any moment.

From white belt to black belt

Dealing with and overcoming bullying is a journey, and most of us start with no knowledge or experience of what's coming. On our programme, we class this as wearing a white belt. We see some parents who have prepared in advance, but most react only after something has happened, and a few don't do anything at all. Either they don't know what to do or don't realise that they have to do something. It is the same with children. The journey we promote to overcoming bullying encompasses three levels of belt: white belt, victim belt and black belt.

We all begin wearing white belts. We come into the world fresh, naive and enthusiastic. We go to school, sports clubs and other places with a perception that anything is possible. We are eager to learn, to do activities, to play. We often have role models we look up to and set out to achieve what they have achieved.

The victim belts are worn by the children and adults who, as a result of the things that have happened to them and how they responded to them, have experienced one or more of the three misery moments. They are easily offended and worry about what people think of them, negative stories playing in their head. When they get feedback, they focus on the negative. Victim belt wearers often play it small, stay in the safe zone and are constantly on the look-out for possible threats. Or they can be ambitious and driven but their low self-confidence and negative self-image limit their ability to perform. Often, they are perfectionists because they need to eliminate all possible criticism. They are so occupied with trying to be perfect that they forget to be in the present moment and enjoy life. There are also people who, though they may not be wearing a victim belt, have a victim stripe in one or two areas, where something has broken them, and are unable to live life to the full in those areas.

BULLYING BREAKTHROUGH 5: NANCY

I was the youngest of four cousins, with our mothers dressing us in matching outfits. Being the youngest, I was always told what to do. I believe this was the root of my lack of confidence. I had no voice and no freedom. This disruption in forming my own identity, I later realised, was what led to my being bullied and living the life of a victim. Something that may seem innocent was a seed planted in my mind for the belief systems I would live by moving forward.

Looking back at this dynamic more than thirty years later, my cousins and I laugh about it. But looking at patterns in my life, I realise that it shaped the person I am today. Bullying looks different in each situation, but the root cause of mine was me not knowing my worth and not having clarity on my identity.

For example, in my fifth grade in school, my friends and I were playing outside after lunch. All of a sudden, I heard a group of boys laughing and looking over at us. Something in my gut told me it wasn't good. I remember feeling nervous as the boys walked over to us. One boy said loudly to me, 'Nancy, you're so skinny. You're flat, too. Flat like an ironing board.' My face turned red from embarrassment and all the other boys laughed even louder.

That boy never knew the impact his comment had on my life. It was another seed planted in my mind that fed a belief system around not being good enough. From that day forward, I began to develop a body complex. 'I'm skinny and unattractive. No man will ever want me.'

I dedicated myself to my studies. Being studious and smart gave me something to hang onto; it became a part of my identity and my comfort zone. I was never going to be seen as attractive but at least I was smart. This seed did two things in my mind: it confirmed that I had no voice, because I didn't stand up for myself, and it created a victim mentality.

This victim mentality forced me to do things that no one ever knew about. In my high school years (age fourteen to sixteen), I would make sure I sat at the front of the class so I couldn't see anyone else. In my mind, sitting at the front helped me to focus on the teacher and the homework. The reality was that I didn't want to be seen, so no one could pick on me.

The bullying didn't stop at school and my breaking point came during my second year of university. I had decided to move away and attend school in another state where no one knew me. For the first three months of the school year, I was depressed. I had no new friends and was missing home. One day, I said to myself, "This is enough. I have to get out of my comfort zone, start talking to people and make some friends." And I did just that. I met some amazing friends that I still have today. It felt so good to finally break free.

This began a ripple effect of change. I started making choices from an empowered state, which led me to crave growth. I hired a mentor to help me get to the root cause of my problems and navigate the changes I wanted to make.

Reaching my breaking point was a pivotal moment, but I had to understand what was happening to break free from it. I didn't want to be a victim anymore. I wanted to reframe all that pain and turn it into something bigger than me.

To do that, I had to face a lot of issues I had hidden away. A critical one was learning to love myself and redefine my self-worth. Once this clicked, I was able to recognise the amazing opportunity I had and start to help others who want to make a similar change.

The pain of my bullying provided my purpose in what I do today. Today, I am a confidence coach and corporate trainer. I participate in keynote speaking events and enjoy helping professionals turn up the volume on their dreams and lead with confidence. I overcame the bullying, forgave myself and everyone involved, and now teach a system that aids in self-empowerment.

Nancy is a great example of someone who, for a time, was stuck wearing a victim belt but, through a journey of self-acceptance and overcoming her bullying, was able to become a black belt wearer. This book, and our work more generally, is about enabling both parents and children to progress from wearing a white belt to a black belt, without putting on the victim belt. There are a few key differences between victim belts and black belts.

Traction vs distraction

The first difference relates to mindset. What does the wearer of a victim belt focus on compared to a black belt? A black belt wearer has their mind set on a goal and makes what life puts in their way, go their way. They don't look at what's happening and wish it were different. They stay on track; they maintain traction.

The wearer of a victim belt is often distracted, wishing things were different. They focus on an imagined future where everything will be better or try to solve their problems through tricks and short-cuts, such as 'get rich quick' schemes. They often follow the latest trend, whether in clothes, diets or sports, and when things don't work out, or don't change as quickly as they'd hoped, they are disappointed. They persuade themselves that they are a loser, that they are 'not meant for this', and avoid trying similar things in the future. This keeps them safe – in a position they often don't like but that is, at least, familiar. This prevents them from gaining traction on the way to achieving their goals.

The victim belt wearer seldom realises that the black belt was often dealt a similar hand in life, but instead of focusing on external quick fixes, they focused on the steps they needed to take in that moment, however hard or uncomfortable it might be. The path to worthwhile achievements is never easy.

Life paths

Due to their different mindsets, people who wear the victim belt and the black belt will have quite different life paths. We picture the different stages in a person's life through the lens of someone who wears a victim belt or a black belt. These images are based on our research, accounts we have heard in our interviews, or on our own experiences.

Elementary school

Victim belt: They feel sick thinking about going to school and hide before school starts to avoid being seen by the bullies. They don't go outside in breaks. They have a hard time concentrating, don't dare to raise their hand even if they know the answer, and perform below their ability. They come home from school in a sad and often aggressive mood.

Black belt: They look forward to going to school. They're outside playing during breaks. They raise their hand when they know the answer or when they have a question. They can focus easily and work hard to improve. They come home with stories and questions.

High school

Victim belt: They don't look forward to changing schools but hope there will be no bullies at high school. They avoid doing school work and continue to be low achievers, always afraid that they might fail. They often receive negative feedback from teachers, who say they lack ability.

Black belt: They continue to perform well and so have more and better options when it comes to choosing their university or college.

Sports/activities/hobbies

Victim belt: They are often reluctant to participate because they are afraid of being bullied. Sometimes, the opposite occurs: this is the place where they feel safe and can progress.

Black belt: They regard these activities as an opportunity to pursue their passion, to challenge their body and mind.

University

Victim belt: They find it hard to live by themselves. They are scared to travel alone, go to certain new places, meet new people and do new things. They are less likely to socialise and party, except within a specific, safe group. They are slower to progress, or focus only on studying. They may quit before they finish because they are afraid of failure.

Black belt: They look forward to a new chapter in their lives. They have built the resilience to live independently and to travel alone. They introduce themselves to new groups, people and activities.

Work

Victim belt: They find it hard to apply for jobs and they procrastinate. They are nervous during job interviews and accept any role they are offered instead of going after their dream job. They have a hard time making acquaintances with colleagues and asking questions because they lack confidence. They may ask others to check their work even if they know it's good but are easily offended and take it personally when given feedback. They think people are talking about them, even if they are not, and don't stand up for themselves. They often become perfectionists in their work and neglect other areas of their life. They will stay in a job they don't like because safety is preferable to uncertainty. They pretend to be someone they're not. They are less likely to save and more likely to buy things they can't afford or get into debt trying to make themselves look the part and impress people they often don't even like.

Black belt: They aspire to a job they love. They don't put off applying and, although they may be nervous at the interview, they go for it. They aren't afraid to speak up and ask questions when they need to. If they feel they can't add anything more in their role or progress further, they look for another job. They are more likely to earn a higher salary and save money, which they spend on experiences, not things.

Relationships

Victim belt: They are scared to approach potential partners because of a fear of rejection. They have a lower chance of meeting a significant other because they tend to go to the same places and meet the same people. Once in a relationship, they try to please their partner and don't stand up for themselves. They are afraid to share and show vulnerability, shying away from confrontation because they don't want to get hurt. They often pick the wrong partners (for example married, abusive, criminal) and try to heal their partner's flaws, staying too long in the wrong relationship.

Black belt. They are confident in approaching potential partners, knowing that being rejected is normal, that you don't always find love straightaway. They dare to share and are vulnerable and honest. They will stand up for themselves and won't stay in the wrong relationship longer than necessary.

Family and children

Victim belt: They try to protect their child from getting hurt by solving their problems for them, preventing the child from becoming self-reliant. They are overprotective, wanting their child to dress and behave in a certain way because they falsely believe this will stop them from being bullied, influencing their child's choices (eg what they should study) because they think they know better. They try to be the 'perfect' parent and best friend. They have excessively high expectations, praising results over effort.

Black belt: They prepare their child to also become a black belt, creating the space for their child to develop, praising their hard work and effort over results.

Retirement

Victim belt: They are more likely to have long-term illnesses. They find it harder to enjoy their retirement, either for health reasons or because they have low energy and feel insecure. They are more likely to have to live on a lower income.

Black belt: They are more likely to stay healthy and live longer. They have more energy, the capability to enjoy life, and often more money to live on.

Attitudes and behaviours

Throughout life, the victim belt and the black belt also have contrasting attitudes and behaviours.

Language

Victim belt: When faced with a challenge, the victim belt will say (or think), 'What if I lose/fail?' 'What if it hurts?' 'What will someone else say or think?' 'I'm no good at that.' 'I can't.' 'I'm a loser.' They make excuses to avoid taking responsibility for the outcome.

Black belt: The black belt takes responsibility: 'I can do that.' 'I have nothing to lose.' 'I will either succeed or learn.' But they are also honest with themselves: 'I can't do that yet.'

Self-control

Victim belt: They are more likely to have a short fuse, finding it harder to deal with emotions, both in themselves and others. They don't handle stress well and may become bullies themselves. They are more likely to have sleep disorders, so that during the day they feel tired and have no energy.

Black belt: They can regulate their emotions and handle stressful situations, with a higher level of tolerance. They are more likely to be able to switch between alertness and relaxation when needed.

Health and happiness

Victim belt: They often hope to find joy in the next thing: 'I'll (allow myself to) be happy when I have that new car, that six-pack, that holiday, etc.' They make unhealthy choices, running a greater risk of metabolic disease and are prone to long-term illness. They tend to be more prone to substance abuse (alcohol, drugs, obsessive hobbies, risk-taking).[26]

Black belt: They make good decisions regarding their health, are generally in better shape and have a lower chance of suffering from addiction.

---

26 L Khoury et al., 'Substance use, childhood traumatic experience, and Posttraumatic Stress Disorder in an urban civilian population', *Depression & Anxiety*, 27/12 (Dec 2010), 1077-1086, www.ncbi.nlm.nih.gov/pmc/articles/PMC3051362, accessed 8 May 2021

Decision-making

Victim belt: They are more likely to base a decision on how they feel at that moment, go for instant gratification and to go for the safe option. They are more likely to make poor decisions, which they will blame on others or on luck.

Black belt: They are better at making the right decisions, where there is delay gratification. If they make a mistake, they find it easier to correct and redirect.

According to carer Bronnie Ware,[27] the five most common regrets people at the ends of their lives have are:

1. I wish I'd had the courage to live a life true to myself, rather than the life others expected of me.

2. I wish I hadn't worked so hard.

3. I wish I'd dared to express my feelings.

4. I wish I'd stayed in touch with my friends.

5. I wish I'd allowed myself to be happier.

What do you notice about this list? They all fit the language of a victim belt.

---

27 B Ware, 'Regrets of the Dying', Bronnie Ware Blog (no date), https://bronnieware.com/blog/regrets-of-the-dying, accessed 7 May 2021

Imagine for a moment what would happen if you swapped a child wearing a black belt in resilience and a child wearing a victim belt, so that they were living each other's lives. Do you think the victim belt wearer would start living like a black belt, or that the black belt would suddenly become (and remain) a victim? No. The black belt wearer would see the victim belt's life in a completely different light. Their focus would be totally different. What to the victim belt wearer were obstacles, to the black belt wearer would be opportunities. If there were any real barriers, the black belt would find ways to break through them.

Best practice

We are often asked by parents why they should do anything about bullying. It's not their fault; it's the parents of the bully that should be doing something, or the school. Unfortunately, most schools and other organisations that try to help make costly mistakes. Here is a list of common, but ineffective, strategies and attitudes we see in both schools and parents.

Creating the right atmosphere: This is a flawed idea because it doesn't take into account what happens outside of this environment. If a child hasn't learned how to change their state, they will be unable to deal with challenges outside any 'safe' environment that is created.

More education and awareness: Many schools will have something like an annual 'anti-bullying day' when a speaker is invited to talk on the subject, or a leaflet is handed out to parents. This is rather like telling people that smoking is bad for you. We already know. We can find all the information we want about bullying; what we need to know about is implementation of strategies and building resilience. We need to teach children to read and regulate their own state and to develop the skills to cope with and even benefit from bullying.

Tougher school rules: Some schools will require parents or students to sign an anti-bullying contract, but it's highly unlikely that this will stop bullying. Instead, we need to make sure that our child has the skills to break through it, if and when it does occur.

Talking to bullies' parents: This is an option, and it might help to stop the bullying. But the damage could already have been done; your child's image of themselves may already be affected. If you stand up for your child, they won't learn how to stand up for themselves. In addition, a child is a bully for a reason, which is often not addressed by this approach, so the cycle of bullying can continue.

Not giving attention to bullies: Some believe that if we don't react to bullying, it will go away. But bullies don't bully to get attention, so this won't stop them. If your child doesn't know how to defend themselves against bullying, it will still affect them even if they try to ignore it.

Encouraging witnesses to speak up: If those who witness bullying try to do something about it, the bullying might stop in that moment. But, again, neither the bully nor the child being bullied will have learned anything and no healing can take place.

'**We must stop bullying':** Bullying can't be completely prevented. The best answer is to develop your child's ability to defend themselves against it and end the cycle of bullying. The bully should not just be stopped but helped to break through bullying themselves.

'**I don't need to do anything; the bullying has already stopped':** We have found that even forty years after suffering bullying, people can still be affected by it. As we have seen, bullying is not a one-off event and, if not dealt with properly, it can have lasting consequences long after it has stopped.

9

A Lot To Look Forward To

People want freedom, for example financial freedom, so they can do the things they want to do. But freedom, and who we are free to become, depends not on what happens to us, but on how we respond to it. To achieve the right response, we need help and support: there is no such a thing as self-made success. No one achieves their full potential on their own. Two people always know more than one. You can see this everywhere, from sports to business, from music to education, where there are teachers and coaches to guide and mentor. On our own, we often become side-tracked, distracted, discouraged or stop when it gets hard. There is great benefit in surrounding yourself with like-minded people who are going through, or have gone through, the same thing as you. When you see someone else succeed, it suddenly feels more possible.

This also applies to your child. When they are in a safe, supporting environment in which they see others break through obstacles, where they are free to be themselves, where they can be vulnerable and progress through chosen and given challenges, they will excel. It also applies to us as parents. We often see parents who are suddenly faced with bullying feeling uncertain. They don't know what to do, how to solve this problem. They can't sleep at night for worrying about it. They might come up with a possible solution, but it is unlikely that it will work completely. They might eventually succeed through trial and error, but this can be costly and time-consuming.

Who, not how

When trying to figure out how to navigate a difficult situation, it's much better to ask a 'who' than a 'how' question. Who has faced this problem and been able to solve it successfully? Who knows more than me about this subject? Who can guide me through the steps, so that I don't miss the blind spots and make unnecessary mistakes?

Answering these questions will save you time, energy and money. Even though technology has enabled so much progress over the last century, eliminating many common chores, we seem to be busier and more time-poor than ever. Parents feel a lot of pressure to play multiple roles: of employee or business owner, household manager, partner, friend, child of their own parents... When they're faced with an additional role, such as mentor or healer, it is common for them to say, 'I don't have time for that', 'I don't have the energy for that', 'It's too hard' or, 'It'll take too long'.

The best way to maximise your time is to seek help and advice from people who have relevant knowledge and experience. Just as we have seen that our child can be helped to use the resources, they have at their disposal more effectively and to make better decisions, it's important we as parents also become more resourceful and efficient in our decision-making.

Beyond a black belt

Once your child has a black belt in resilience, you will feel proud – but also sad, because your role will have changed, from mentor to observer. You will be able to step back and trust your child to make their own decisions, so that they can build trust in themselves. Of course, at this stage, we must continue to support our child and show kindness and understanding. We must cement the lessons we and they have learned from the 6Ps. Most importantly, though, we must focus on developing their character.

Character: The 3Cs

A child's character is the most important aspect of their education and growth, but it's often the missing ingredient in their development. We can sum a child's character up using the 3Cs: their conduct, confidence, and their concentration (with the possibility of a fourth C – Community). It's their ability to set and achieve goals, to have a vision, to develop a strong moral compass. Their ability to step out of their comfort zone and seek challenge and adventure. It's their integrity, their indomitable spirit. It guides every decision they make and ultimately sets them up for a happy and successful life as an adult.

For this reason, we believe that the focus of a child's growth should be on their character, not their academic success. A child with a strong character won't need to be pushed to achieve good grades; they will be intrinsically motivated to achieve on their own. Their mature outlook on life and their higher emotional IQ will ensure that they grow rapidly in all areas. Where the focus has been on academic success as the main indicator of a child's overall development, we have often witnessed little carry-over into the development of their character.

We've mentored over 8,000 children and discovered that every child has a breakthrough area in their character. This is an area of focus that, once developed to a high level, results in rapid development of a child's character. A breakthrough area is typically one of the 3Cs (conduct, confidence, concentration). A child will often have high levels of one, sometimes of two, but rarely of all three. By developing all three to a high level, a child achieves what we call a black belt character, which will ultimately set them up for a successful and happy life as an adult. Let's look at each area in turn:

Conduct

Showing respect and courtesy and having a high level of self-control are vital to developing a young person's character. Children with good conduct are far less likely to be swayed by negative peer pressure and make bad decisions as they grow up. They are also more likely to form strong, happy relationships as adults, as they will have greater empathy and understanding of other people's emotions.

One of the most significant discoveries we made when looking at improving the conduct of young people is the impact it has on relationships at home. Parents of children who have excellent conduct spend less time disciplining them and reinforcing rules over and over again. Instead, the time they have together as a family is spent enjoying each other's company and creating meaningful connections that improve communication, empathy and gratitude, and helps them stay close.

Confidence

Confidence is vital for success and happiness in life, and fundamental to the development of character. Young people with high levels of confidence are more likely to take up challenges and step out of their comfort zone than those with low confidence, which means they develop and learn far quicker. There is a compounding effect where growth becomes exponential rather than linear.

Many parents make the mistake of pushing their child too much, taking them too far out of their comfort zone, which can cause high levels of anxiety and limit progress. On the other hand, some parents don't push their children enough, due to fear of them being hurt, emotionally or physically. There is an ideal place between these two extremes, the 'optimal performance zone' that we discussed in chapter two.

Concentration

Concentration is one of the greatest challenges for young people, particularly today when there are so many distractions all around us. But the ability to concentrate is a vital part of a child's character. A child who is able to concentrate and focus will be able to apply themselves to complicated tasks and learn quickly. This positively impacts their grades at school and so will also have a profound effect on their confidence levels. When a child is able to concentrate and perform a task well, they will enjoy the process of learning more; this again has a compounding effect that will ultimately determine the level of success they achieve in life.

Community

As we have discussed, the community in which a child is immersed is also vital to the development of their character. We might consider this the fourth C, though in a sense it's the foundation of the three, making it vital. A positive, supportive community will be the springboard from which your child launches themselves into adulthood.

Your child will be far more likely to step out of their comfort zone and build their confidence if they know their community is there to support them. If their community is goal-orientated, setting and achieving goals together and celebrating wins, they will grow quickly. More importantly, though, they will understand the process of growth, which will stay with them for life.

If your child is part of a close-knit community with a strong mentor, they will have the consistent support required to guide them through the three big transitions of childhood (changing school, adolescence, and loss/separation), transitions that can make or break your child's character.

If the community your child is a part of has a strong moral code, they will quickly learn and understand values such as respect, courtesy and integrity. This will have a huge impact on their emotional intelligence and their ability to form and maintain meaningful relationships.

Focusing on each of these four Cs, though particularly your child's breakthrough area, using the methods we have talked about will undoubtedly bring about a dramatic improvement in your child's character.

Conclusion

In this book, we've delved into our own stories and shown the impact bullying has had on our lives. We've also shared the stories of successful individuals who attribute part of their success to the bullying they have experienced. These stories show how, while bullying can be traumatic, with the correct mentoring and emotional healing, we can capitalise on the experience. The pain we suffer through bullying can become our strength and propel us forward in life with a higher emotional IQ, deeper relationships and a better outlook on life.

Some children will be deeply scarred by bullying, setting them up to adopt victim-like behaviour, shying away from challenges. A lot of children who have been bullied can start to bully themselves and carry insecurities with them that they pass on to their children. Others will break through the bullying, setting them up with capability and resilience to take on the challenges they will face as they go through life. We believe that this depends on how we prepare our child, through teaching and training, to handle obstacles whether physical, mental, emotional or social.

When we are born, we don't know anything. Everything needs to be learned by doing, often by falling, getting up and starting again with a little more knowledge and skill. As parents, we also learn on the hoof. Often, this can be overwhelming and stressful. In this book, we have shown you ways to overcome this and explained how preparation changes perception and enables you to react faster and better.

We live in a time where technology is progressing faster than ever, when knowledge is increasing at an unprecedented rate, but when people's ability to protect their health and vitality, to cope with and overcome problems, is declining. More than ever, we need to invest time, energy and money into our child's future. It won't be easy, but it will be worth it. Remember, it is far better to be proactive and prepare your child than to deal with a problem reactively; far better to teach them to overcome challenges than to protect them from them altogether, or to solve problems for them.

You picked up this book for a reason: you are ready to act. Now is the time to give your child a black belt in resilience for a head start in life. This book will guide you – we hope it will be a valuable companion on your journey.

Resources

Books

Bates, S, *The Warrior Method* (Rethink Press, 2018)

Polly, M, *American Shaolin: Flying Kicks, Buddhist Monks and the Legend of Iron Crotch* (Gotham, 2007)

Polly, M, *Bruce Lee: A Life* (Simon and Schuster, 2018)

Polly, M, *Tapped Out: Rear naked chokes, the octagon and the last Emperor: An odyssey in mixed martial arts* (Gotham, 2012)

Online resources

Breakthrough Bullying Scorecard: Score yourself and your child on the 6Ps of the Not A Victim process. You'll receive a customised report and steps you can take to speed up your progress. Go to: www.notavictim.co.uk

Daily Black Belt Resilience Journal: Includes a daily morning and evening ritual, with exercises, a progress tracker and a section for recording stories relating to resilience and things you want to remember. For more information visit: www.notavictim.co.uk

Facebook Online Support Group: A friendly community of parents who share their experiences and provide support, inspiration and hope: www.facebook.com/groups/notavictimsupportgroup

Not A Victim: A wealth of resources including a cyberbully app, body language assessment, incident log template, community analyser and social media contract. Go to: www.notavictim.co.uk

The Parable of Dory, a bedtime story about building resilience. For more information visit www.notavictim.co.uk/books

Siebinga, M, 'Superagers', Apple Podcasts Preview (April 2021), https://podcasts.apple.com/nl/podcast/vergeet-oud-te-worden/id1530542130, accessed 8 May 2021

Courses and programmes

For more information on all the following programmes, visit: www.notavictim.co.uk

Not A Victim Anti-Bullying Workshop: A more
detailed exploration of the six-step Not A Victim process described in this book.

Anti-Bullying Summit: Brings together experts
across a broad section of fields including psychology,
traditional education, occupational therapy, character
development, cybersafety and martial arts to provide
parents with deep insights into bullying as well as
practical advice.

Not A Victim Black Belt Resilience Programme: Our
real-time, three- to six-month training programme
to equip you with everything you need to guide and
mentor your child to a black belt in resilience.

Get A Head Start Programme: A programme to build
mental health, resilience and peak performance.
Includes our clinically validated app that allows you
to measure, monitor and guide your child to peak
mental fitness. Voted among the best in the world by
the Bill and Melinda Gates Foundation, it has been
shown to be effective in over twenty clinical trials.

Acknowledgements

We would like to thank all the individuals and experts who have contributed with their work to our research, discoveries and understanding, particularly Brian Mackenzie, Emily Hightower, Shift Adapt, Andrew Huberman, Keiron Sparrowhawk, Steven Kotler, Jamie Wheal, Tony Blauer, Jane and Kelly McGonigal, John Demartini, Daniel Priestley and the KPI Community, the Warrior Academy Team and community and all of the guests on the Warrior Academy Podcast, the Body & Brein Team and Fawwaz Aziz.

We'd especially like to thank Barry Lee Cummings for contributing to the section on cyberbullying. Barry is one of the world's leading cybersafety experts and co-founder of 'Beat the Cyberbully', an application that delivers up-to-date content on the subjects of cyber-safety, cyberbullying prevention, social engineering and online reputation management.

We are also indebted to Hetty van Dijk, a retired general practitioner and former student of Menno's father, who contributed content on how the brain works and wrote the inspiring breakthrough stories based on interviews from the Warrior Academy with Jason Graystone and Matthew Polly.

We could not have written this book if it weren't for our martial art mentors over the years. We'd also like to thank our parents for providing us with a safe environment, trust and wisdom.

Finally, we thank our families for their constant support, care and encouragement on this epic journey toward making a global impact on bullying.

The Authors

Sebastian Bates

 Sebastian Bates is the founder of the Warrior Academy, a global martial arts organisation that has been voted among the top five in the UK. The Academy runs programmes all around the world and its clients include the royal family in the UAE. Sebastian is a best-selling author on the subject of character development, having published *The Warrior Method* in 2018, and host of the Warrior Academy Podcast, which was ranked among the top three educational podcasts in the world on iTunes upon its release.

Sebastian Bates

🌐 www.sebastianbates.com

🌐 www.warrioracademy.co.uk

🌐 www.warrioracademy.ae

Menno Siebinga

Menno is a Superagers trainer specialising in unlocking vitality, life and meaning in people over fifty. His business, 'Body & Brein', reinvents aging and vitality using a unique approach to physical and mental training. Menno is co-author of the books *Fit for Leadership 3* and *Retire to Inspire 1* and is working on a new book, *Superagers, the Art and Science of Forgetting to Grow Old*. A trained physiotherapist, Menno is also a former European and world champion in Escrima, as well as co-host of the Warrior Academy Podcast. He also has his own Superagers Podcast.

For more details about the programmes and projects run by Sebastian and Menno, get in touch.

Menno Siebinga

⊕ www.bodyenbrein.nl

⊕ www.superouderen.nl